SPACE FOR MOVEMENT?

Reflections from Bolivia on

climate justice,
social movements
and the state

BUILDING BRIDGES COLLECTIVE

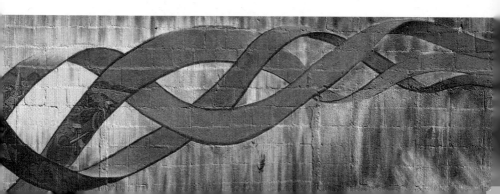

CONTENTS

BOXES

A street - La Paz

1.

"Copenhagen was their 'last chance' — and they failed. Instead, they treated all of our futures as another round of trade negotiations. It is now up to people of the world to take back decision-making power and start making the changes that we urgently need. As climate justice activists based in Europe we welcome the People's Conference as one important step on the long journey towards a post-capitalist society and are happy to have this opportunity to discuss, learn and plan with other climate justice activists around the world" (from our open letter to Participants in the World People's Conference on Climate Change and the Rights of Mother Earth).

INTRODUCTION – A FRESH PATH

Last December's COP-15 climate summit, held in Copenhagen, was the fifteenth Conference of Parties (COP) to the United Nations Framework Convention on Climate Change (UNFCCC). At these annual meetings most of the world's governments come together to negotiate agreements on how they will address the problem of climate change.

In reality, the summit can be seen as a microcosm of our world: a small self-selected elite making deals behind closed doors that will result in widespread destruction, whilst those resisting are either repressed or ignored. The Copenhagen (non)accord was not only a subversion of the apparently democratic process of the United Nations (UN), but many argue that it would also lead the world to a catastrophic 4°C temperature rise by the end of the century.

The failure of the summit was, for many, an unsurprising illustration of governments' and institutions' inability to genuinely address the multiple social and ecological crises that we are facing today. European governments, in conjunction with multinational corporate partners and mainstream NGOs, have responded to evidence of climate chaos by offering false solutions such as carbon trading, biofuels, increased border controls, militarization or investment in nuclear energy. Despite the social, legal and scientific imperatives to act, the (il)logic of economic growth and business as usual marches on.

The thousands of people who took to the streets during COP-15 for 'System Change, not Climate Change!' and to assert a different politics were met with severely repressive policing aimed at preventing any dissent towards global hegemonic powers. This is just another example of the violence that the system needs to impose in order to maintain and expand the status-quo. However, as with the World Trade Organisation international trade negotiations before it, there is growing resistance to this new round of capitalist accumulation, resistance that is coming from within the process;

"Here what is at issue is whether we are going to live or we are going to die, here we are debating if we are going to save lives or we are going to kill. And the differences are very clear in relation to temperatures. If they rise by 2 degrees centigrade then islands of the world, the snows of the Andes mountains and the rest of the world, will be wiped out. It's very serious, and our peoples are not going to accept it, sooner or later they are going to judge it." (Evo Morales Ayma, during the Climate Summit in Copenhagen, December 2009).

Bolivia is a good example of a country where climate change is a very present reality, with associated floods, droughts and melting glaciers threatening the water supply and forced migration from failing agriculture and water scarcity. With strong anti-capitalist speeches and coming from the indigenous social movements, Bolivian president Evo Morales, is leading a coalition of Latin American countries pushing a range of proposals to address the fact that those least responsible for climate change are those already suffering its impacts. This coalition of states identify capitalism as the root cause of climate change and reject market based green capitalist responses, instead proposing a declaration for the rights of Mother Earth and an international court for climate criminals.

Responding to the failure of the UN summit, Morales called for a World Peoples' Conference on Climate Change and the Rights of Mother Earth, (Conferencia Mundial de los Pueblos sobre el Cambio Climatico y Derechos de la Madre Tierra- CMPCC), that took place in Cochabamba from 19th-22nd April 2010. For many, the conference offered a potential new space for developing a new politics. Led by the demands of global social movements, there was an emphasis on a bottom-up process, and it was a space where people with very different experiences, perspectives and struggles could come together to discuss and organise.

This collective writing project is an attempt to make sense of what happened in and around the CMPCC, what it means, and to mark where we think we are in July 2010, six months on from COP-15. We approached this summit as an opportunity to discuss some big questions about climate, capitalism, governments and working together in solidarity. We will explore some of the complex contradictions and share some of what we heard in Bolivia. We have not attempted to provide an apolitical, objective account of the CMPCC (if you believe that such a thing can ever exist), but are explicitly reflecting on this from our anti-authoritarian perspective. We are just as interested in what happened on the edges as what went on in the centre. We will be more questioning, rather than providing clear answers.

As autonomous activists based in Europe, we had several difficult discussions before deciding to participate in the CMPCC. Various factors motivated us to attend; some of us were passionate about particular

WHERE ARE WE COMING FROM AND WHY DID WE GO?

themes in the working groups whilst others of us wanted face-to-face discussions as part of networking for the global day of action call-out for October
12th (see box xi). The summit was a unique opportunity to meet with many
grassroots movements and to hear a much greater range of voices, experiences and perspectives than from those few who have found funding to come
to Europe in the past. We were all concerned that the majority of people attending, in particular those
from Europe, would be from mainstream NGOs and we wanted to balance this with participation from
European-based movements who recognise capitalism, and the political structures that facilitate it, as the
root cause of climate change. A Bolivian commentator had said just before the conference, "There is no
anti-capitalist analysis of climate change in Europe"[1] and we thought it was important to show there was!

Of course this Bolivian analysis of climate change as a systemic problem is by no means unique. For years
people have been aware that humans are pushing the natural environment to breaking point. Whilst the
majority of mainstream environmentalism has not engaged with root causes, there are many more radical
groups, networks and mobilisations around the world who locate climate change as a symptom of the capitalist system, Earth First!, Rising Tide and Camps for Climate Action, to give a few examples. Whilst an exami-
nation of these different perspectives is beyond our remit here, there are links in the resources section where
more information can be found. At the same time, it is important to note that there are those who share
this analysis, but have concluded that we have already passed tipping points, and that trying to 'stop climate
change' is now irrelevant. Others view all climate discourses as co-opted by corporate, state and reformist
NGO rhetoric. As was apparent during the mobilisations in Copenhagen, whilst many share an analysis of the
root causes, (System Change not Climate Change!) there is little consensus on how to move forward.

Linked to this, there were some tough political debates behind our decision to attend. Climate change is a
difficult issue for anti-authoritarian, anti-capitalists to navigate. Certainly in Europe, governments, radical
environmental and social movements, (and increasingly corporations) appear to agree — climate change is
bad and needs to be reversed. Whilst being against climate change is not a political position, discussions
of how we got into this mess and how we can change things certainly bring us back to politics.

Dramatic action is required to mitigate against the devastating consequences of climate change, where
those least responsible for the crisis will disproportionately experience the effects. In light of this, a difficult
question we face is whether the division between those who are prepared to use the state and those who
reject it as part of the problem deserves re-examination, especially within contexts like Bolivia. On one side,
some argue that it is only when we get rid of the state, governments and capital-relations that we can really
begin to deal with climate change and its root causes. On the other are those who feel the urgency of the
situation requires such a diverse and multi-layered approach that it is important to put aside differences and
unite with various actors for the immediate task of reducing emissions. Pitted
against impending tipping points and associated climate chaos, many have
entered into grey political spaces with regards to movement building, strategies and how to position themselves in relation to this complex politics.

‹1› Franz Chávez (2010), "From
Copenhagen to Cochabamba".
IPS news: ipsnews.net/news.
asp?idnews=50851 (retrieved
April 2010)

During the mobilisations against the COP-15 within Climate Justice Action, these thorny issues were bought to the fore. There were a wide spectrum of opinions amongst people and groups in the net-

'SHUT IT DOWN' OR 'SHUT THEM IN'?

work on how to approach the summit, ranging from total disruption of the meetings through to a desire to pressure governments to take radical decisions inside. The arguments were delicate and complicated, precisely because of the impacts that climate change is already having on a large portion of the world's population and the threat of passing climatic tipping points. Many agreed that the UN was simply being used to legitimise the expansion of a green capitalism, with climate change as an excuse. Although often in agreement with this view, others feared that if not the UN, then what?

What became clear in Copenhagen is that despite much work done in the run-up to the meeting, UN climate summits do not yet occupy such a clearly illegitimate position as do the World Bank, International Monetary Fund, G8 and World Trade Organisation. Perhaps this factor can help us to reflect on why such a big mobilisation of people in Copenhagen never quite got it together to take effective action on the scale required.

In light of our decision to participate in a state sponsored conference this question demanded careful consideration. The stated intention of the summit was to identify and discuss the structural causes of climate change, in order to take action and to move the debate away from technical apolitical negotiations. In Bolivia, the clear distinction between social movements and the government is blurred, with many of those now working in the government having been or still being part of inspiring popular struggles,

IS 'OUR' PARTICIPATION GIVING MORE LEGITIMACY TO 'THEIR' ATTEMPTS FOR CO-OPTATION?

most famously the gas and water wars that chucked out multinational corporations and bought down governments (see box iii). Whilst in our work in Europe, direct invitations to work with or within the state are highly improbable and undesired, in regions of Latin America, and Bolivia in particular, the political contexts are quite different. Does the Bolivian government in particular offer any new insights in terms of an effective relationship between social movements and the state? Is Bolivia's government serving as a catalyst for social change, or was the summit an attempt to co-opt radical demands? We think this is worth reflecting on, to develop a better understanding and in order to continue the work of building transnational alliances.

At the same time we knew that in the run-up to the 'People's Summit' active groups in Cochabamba were warned by organisers not to 'cause any trouble.' Alongside radical government discourse there are ongoing struggles against resource extraction and development in Bolivia and many remain cautious of any state led process, even one that calls itself a People's summit. We wanted to find and talk to these critical perspectives and to find out how the Bolivian government's fine words on the international stage were playing out domestically. As it turned out, there was no lack of dissenting voices present inside and around the event.

We begin with the Open Letter, which we distributed both before and during the conference, and

WHAT'S IN THE BOOK?

which we used as the basis for carrying out the interviews and discussions. This letter lays out some of our shared perspectives. Next we outline the historical context in which the Peoples' Summit took place – to understand why it happened in Latin

America, and in Bolivia in particular. Next we explore the term 'climate justice', a concept which many of us first came into contact with through the mobilisations for COP-15 in Copenhagen and which, as we have discovered through this process, can have several different meanings. Next we describe what happened within the processes of the summit, and how we participated whilst there. The main part of the booklet is then divided into five sections, each reflecting upon one of the questions we asked in around twenty interviews, and sharing what we heard from the people we spoke with. Following these analyses, we attempt to reflect on the conference on a number of different levels from its impact on the official UN process to what it might mean for social movements. We finish with some final reflections, and by raising some (more!) questions. Along the way the text is broken up by boxes giving background information or sharing recollections in an attempt to fill in some gaps and bring the story to life. At the back you can find definitions of all the acronyms and other potentially unclear terms that are used, as well as short biographies of the people we interviewed.

We felt that producing this booklet was also important because there was very little coverage of the CMPCC, so it has not been widely heard of, let alone understood. Nick Buxton, media officer for the Peoples' summit, explained that the mainstream media were just not interested as it was a Southern conference without a major power, i.e. Brazil. He said, "Even the sympathetic journalists couldn't get the story covered. They were filing stories but they weren't getting picked up". However, more than just reporting on what happened in and around this conference, we want to open up discussions. Whilst a lot of this feedback will be on-line or face to face between groups and networks, we hope that a written reflection can contribute something to these ongoing conversations by pulling together some different strands of analysis.

We strongly believe that climate change cannot be addressed while it is separated from economic, political and social relations, and our use of and connections to land, food, forests, etc. This booklet is not purely intended for self-defining climate activists, anti-capitalists, socialists, anarchists, environmentalists, students or anti-racists. Instead we hope that it can be of interest to all of the above, and more. We hope that it will promote debate and action and we hope that anyone interested in taking practical action to create a less exploitative and truly sustainable world will find it provides some insight.

DISCLAIMER We returned from spending just under a month in Bolivia in early May. Whilst doing our jobs, our normal activities and trying to maintain our vegetable gardens, we have had regular online meetings to hammer out a collective analysis. We also travelled from our respective homes and spent two intense days working together. For various personal and strategic reasons we wanted to publish this collectively in July. This has, however, meant that not all pieces necessarily fully reflect the views of all of us in the collective. It has been an ambitious project so please excuse the inevitable inconsistencies, repetitions and omissions.

OPEN LETTER TO PARTICIPANTS IN THE WORLD PEOPLE S CONFERENCE ON CLIMATE CHANGE AND THE RIGHTS OF MOTHER EARTH

Following the complete failure of the COP15 and the climate negotiations that came before it, it is clear that the world's governments, their intergovernmental organizations, and the corporations who sit at their tables, are not capable of taking the steps needed to prevent further climate change and the devastation it brings. Copenhagen was their 'last chance' — and they failed. Instead, they treated all of our futures as another round of trade negotiations. It is now up to people of the world to take back decision-making power and start making the changes that we urgently need. As climate justice activists based in Europe we welcome the People's Conference as one important step on the long journey towards a post-capitalist society and are happy to have this opportunity to discuss, learn and plan with other climate justice activists around the world.

Our daily lives are increasingly colonised by capitalism, from the land we use and the shelter we need to the water we drink and the food we eat — in some parts of the world even our laughter has become commodified. We are forced into making decisions based on the logic of profit. From famine, war and oppression to dull and demeaning work, the climate crisis is only the latest symptom of this senseless system of endless economic growth on a finite planet. As usual, the impacts of this crisis will be felt most strongly by those least responsible for causing it.

Meanwhile, so-called 'solutions' to climate change only extend further the arms of business, financiers, and polluters, commodifying the atmosphere itself. It is clear that carbon trading, the Clean Development Mechanism (CDM), and the Reduced Emissions from Deforestation and Forest Degradation (REDD) scheme do not solve the problem but dispossess people of their land and livelihoods while allowing corporations to profit and avoid any real change to their dirty practices. We reject those NGOs that support this insanity whilst claiming to speak 'on behalf of civil society'. These organisations do not represent us and they are not part of the solution. They exist to advise upon the development of a 'green' capitalism. We don't buy the lie!

We believe that only those committed to living and learning true, bottom up solutions can face the challenges of climate change and make the changes that we now urgently need. Together we must ask the questions and learn from our answers. No business can invest in a future we want to be a part of, no governments can make these changes for us. It is time for us to provide for ourselves, to find new ways to relate to each other and the world around us, and to be able to live without fear of persecution. In order to stop further climate chaos, movements and peoples need to take back control over our own lives.

Those with wealth and power, predominantly based in the geographic Global North, have a legacy of centuries of exploitation of labour and natural resources, and a vicious system of racism and exclusion. We see that national armies and the police exist primarily to preserve this current order. In contrast to this, we aim to work on principles of solidarity, autonomy, cooperation and direct action. We are working to radically change our relationship to the food and energy we produce and consume, and to leave fossil fuels in the ground. We believe in freedom of movement for people and ideas — not capital.

We have come here to listen, discuss and learn, so that together we can see how these principles can be extended into all spheres of life. As people living in Europe involved in small but growing social movements, we want to deepen conversations and dialogue with the rich variety of different experiences here in Cochabamba. Later, we wish to take these ideas back to where we live, to share, to continue the processes of learning in our communities and ultimately build bonds between movements across the world. We have been inspired by what has been achieved in various global struggles. At the same time, we know we constantly need to question where we are going. For these reasons we would like to discuss with you the following questions:

- Do you think that the UNFCC and the COP process can be effectively used to bring about climate justice? If so, how?

- Is climate justice possible without moving beyond capitalist relations?

- What are the possibilities and dangers of social movements cooperating with governments and the state?

- What does solidarity mean, and how can we work together more effectively to build the transnational struggle for climate justice? What are your views on the 'global south' and 'global north' and their relationships to struggle?

In solidarity,

The February gathering of Climate Justice Action (CJA),
Amsterdam.

A view of the Andes

2.

After fifteen years of ineffective international climate negotiations the UNFCCC's so-called 'Copenhagen Accord' was the only non-agreement to come out of the 2009 COP-15. Formulated by a closed group of

SITUATING THE CONFERENCE

26 political leaders, it was opposed by the governments of Venezuela, Nicaragua, Bolivia, Sudan and Tuvalu, who rejected not only its undemocratic creation but also its weak content with no binding obligations for industrialised countries to reduce their emissions and placing heavier mitigation commitments on

developing countries. This three-page document was not officially adopted by the Conference of Parties (COP) but was only 'taken note of'. Despite this, the Obama administration has been negotiating the (non) accord outside the UN process, denying developing countries access to climate aid if they refused to sign onto it. Additionally, the constant pressure from powerful interests to establish this document as the starting point for further negotiations is deeply problematic. In response, and supported by the emerging leadership of a counter-block with 'progressive' governments in Latin America, Evo Morales called for the CMPCC. It was no coincidence that Cochabamba would host the Peoples' Conference as it is central for Bolivia's struggles that became world renowned ten years ago during the 'water war' (see box iii). Neither was it a coincidence that Morales, the first Indigenous president of Bolivia and coming from the social movements, was the only president who could make a successful call for a People's Summit.

However, before we delve deeper into the details of the CMPCC, it is important to explore some of the historical economic, political and social struggles of the region in order to understand the complexities and messy politics between movements and the state that are currently at play in Bolivia. By giving a general outline of the Latin American and Bolivian context we can get a better understanding of the challenges that the region's movements are facing. This section doesn't intend to cover all Latin American struggles, that would be impossible here, but is an attempt to map some key issues that could help us better understand the current politics.

LATIN AMERICA:

Throughout the history of Latin America different waves of occupation, dispossession and increasing political repression gave birth to strong waves of resistance. During the colonial period, the Indigenous Tupac Katari, Bartolina Sisa and Tupac Amaru led strong confrontations against the colonial powers. While Katari and Sisa fought to overthrow the Spanish authorities taking control of the city of La Paz in 1781, Amaru fought for the abolishment of Indigenous slavery and the payments to the Spanish crown in Peru. Although the revolution did not materialise back then, the rebel spirits were far from being stopped. As Katari said before he was killed: "I will be back and I will be millions."

Once the majority of the countries got independence at the beginning of the nineteenth century, new forms of empire entered the region led by the US and its corporations. Peasants, workers, students and entire families resisted this new form of colonialism all over again. A key moment was when the revolutionary Che Guevara, together with Fidel Castro, led the Cuban Revolution which overthrew the US-supporter, Fulgencio Batista, in 1959. Che Guevara still brings hope and pride to revolutionaries in Latin America, and especially to Bolivia where he was killed in 1967 while trying to ignite another revolution.

During the 70s, the cheap dollar in the world capital markets made it possible for many developing countries to run-up huge debts, which had to be paid at increased interest rates after the shift in economic policies from Keynesian to neoliberal. At the same time, the Cold War offered the US a pretext to support dictators in order to facilitate the exploitation of resources and people and tie them into free market economies. Proxy wars were also common at this time as the two superpowers (the USSR and the US) did not want to run the risk of escalation to a nuclear war. In this sense, many Latin American governments were controlled from offices in Washington. The US, for example, supported the dictatorship in Argentina (1976 – 1983) that left thousands dead and stirred opposition from, among others, the *Madres de la Plaza de Mayo*, demanding justice for the disappeared. At the same time, in Chile the socialist Salvador Allende won the elections in 1970. After three years of attacks from the CIA, the General Augusto Pinochet perpetrated a *coup d'état* and ruled a dictatorship for 16 years. While Pinochet opened the door for the 'Chicago Boys' to apply neoliberal policies, the brutal repression left thousands of people killed, victims of torture, and unknown numbers disappeared. Most of the region fell in the 80s in what came to be known as the 'lost decade', being particularly true for countries such as Argentina, Bolivia, Mexico and Peru, where these policies had deep impacts on the marginalised sectors of societies.

With Latin America at the frontline of the neoliberal project, the hegemony of the 'Washington Consensus' in the mid-90s, a set of policies promoted by the International Monetary Fund (IMF) and the World Bank (WB), gave a green light to free trade, tax reforms, liberalisation of labour markets, and privatisation of public companies. The governmental budgets for education, health and public transport were drastically cut. As a result, the middle classes and elites started to integrate into and benefit from the global markets, while the marginalised majority suffered from structural inequality, oppression and repression.

In Venezuela the 1989 IMF riots, known as the *"Caracazo"* marked a turning point in the struggle against neoliberalism. The uprising against President Carlos Andres Pérez, who implemented the economic 'shock' policies, was triggered by a huge boost in petrol prices and a new economic austerity programme. The protests went on for days of intense resistance, repression and killing of civilians. The *Caracazo* sparked struggles that went on throughout the 90s and resulted in the 1998 electoral win of the current president, Hugo Chávez, who promised a 'twenty-first-century socialism.'

In the same decade, when 'free trade' gained terrain in 1994 with the signing of the North American Free Trade Agreement (NAFTA) treaty between the US, Canada and Mexico, the *Ejército Zapatista de Liberación Nacional* (EZLN) began a rebellion in Chiapas, Mexico. In opposition to the neoliberal agenda they demanded the rights of self-determination for all peoples. This struggle for autonomy for Mexican peasants has inspired millions around the world. In 1996, they called for an 'International Gathering for Humanity and against Neo-Liberalism' where more than 3000 people gathered in the forests of Chiapas to discuss alternative worlds.

A few years later in Argentina, during the economic crises of 2001, workers occupied hotels, bankrupted factories and business to form cooperatives. Mass street protests forced the president Fernando de la Rua to resign and in the following days Argentina had a succession of four different presidents as movements forced out one president after another. Today, there are around 200 factories and businesses run as cooperatives with more than 15 thousand workers involved.

There are thousands of other examples of strong Latin American opposition to the neoliberal project; Landless movements in Brazil and Paraguay; armed guerillas in El Salvador, Guatemala, Nicaragua, Perú and Colombia; Indigenous resistance in Ecuador, Bolivia and Perú; uprisings in Oaxaca, Mexico; the *'piqueteros'* movements in Argentina; and the water and gas wars in Bolivia, to name but a few. Since the beginning of the 90s the movements have overthrown two presidents in Ecuador and Argentina, and one each in Paraguay, Perú and Brazil, and collapsed corrupted systems in Venezuela and Perú. These uprisings have opened the door for electoral victories by the left in Venezuela, Bolivia, Nicaragua, Honduras, El Salvador, Paraguay, Brazil and Ecuador, a swing that is sometimes referred to as the Pink Tide.

However, Latin America is far from being a joint block. The existence of strong political powers like Brazil and Venezuela creates a new set of regional power relations. Perú and Colombia on the other hand, both with a history of armed guerrillas, civil wars and US-intervention through the 'war on drugs', are still governed by the extreme right and are the two closest allies of the US in the region.

The challenges for Latin America are crucial in the years to come for the process of a real transformation. This is especially true for the changing relationships between social movements and the state. 'Progressive' governments have started to articulate social movements' agendas. The words 'anti-imperialism', 'anti-capitalism' and 'anti-colonialism' form part of every speech from the ALBA governments. While it was the resistance against the neoliberal project that allowed these presidents to come to power, these same presidents are now re-legitimising the existence of the state itself, while continuing capitalist forms of development. The co-optation of movements and leaders to calm social unrest is a very dangerous and real consequence. It is true however that significant parts of the movements have not stopped fighting for their autonomy and are re-articulating spaces of struggle and their relationships with the state within current Latin American politics.

ii.
REGIONAL INTEGRATION AND ALLIANCE OF BOLIVARIAN STATES (ALBA)

The Bolivarian Alliance for the Peoples of the Americas (ALBA) is an alternative political, economic and social integration block among countries of Latin America and the Caribbean. It was created as a counter hegemonic block to the free trade model of neoliberal globalisation. ALBA's founding principles commit to a "firm rejection of the content and goals of the FTAA (Free Trade Agreement of the Americas)" which was pushed by the US. It instead affirms that "the cardinal principle that should guide ALBA is the great solidarity among the people of Latin America and the Caribbean."

Its member nations are the founding countries Cuba and Venezuela (2004), Bolivia (2006), Nicaragua (2007), Dominica (2008), Ecuador (2009), Saint Vincent and the Grenadines (2009), and Antigua and Barbuda (2009). Haiti and Uruguay are 'observer states', which are not official members but are included in regional conferences.

By trying to limit the role of transnational corporations and reclaiming public control over hydrocarbons, the ALBA governments have started to gain more control over the powerful energy sector. However, in Venezuela and Bolivia this has materialised in 'mixed' contracts between private and public investments, with states having the majority participation.

Bolivia joined ALBA in 2006 and proposed the creation of a People's Trade Treaty (*Tratado de Comercio de los Pueblos* – TCP) aimed for a "Just and sustainable endogenous development based on communal principles". The ALBA-TCP has implemented many equity-based exchanges between Cuba, Venezuela and Bolivia, taking into consideration the asymmetries among these countries. For example, Cuba offered Bolivia six ophthalmology centres, 20 hospitals, 600 doctors and nurses, and 5,000 medicine scholarships for Bolivian students to study in Cuba. Venezuela supplies oil, fuels and asphalt to Bolivia in exchange for Bolivian products, and offers technological assistance to the public companies dealing with oil and mining. Bolivia on the other hand has less material contributions: it offers mainly experience for holistic researches on Indigenous peoples, natural medicines and biodiversity.

During the 2008 ALBA meeting, the *'Consejo de Movimientos Sociales'* (CMS) or Social Movement Council, was created in order to construct spaces for popular participation in the creation of alternative policies for regional integration. The social movements of each ALBA country are responsible for its national organization and it aims to include movements from other countries of the Americas. Although the CMS is still in an initial phase, the CMS-Venezuela is already articulating debates and proposals among movements and social organizations. In front of the Peoples' Summit they presented a documented that stated: "We believe in the construction of a socialism that fights and prioritise the transformation of all relations of domination and oppression. Our proposals, as peoples, have to be radical. It has to be a call for a frontal fight against the dominant system. Here we are to meet, reflect, conclude, and take a militant perspective... We recognise ALBA as a space for construction, exchange and articulation among the peoples that take part of it, understanding from this not only the national states that are part of ALBA but also all the movements and social organizations of our América and the rest of the world."[2]

The president of Honduras, Manuel Zelaya, joined the ALBA block in 2008. The congress led by Roberto Micheletti, who later became the de facto president after the coup d'état in 2009, approved ALBA the same year. This addition allowed Honduras among other things to get access to low-interest credits and preferable prices for the acquisition of oil. In December 2009, Micheletti took state power and perpetrated violent repression against the social movements who opposed the coup. The Honduran congress, controlled by coup supporters from the centrist Liberal Party and other right wing parties, met in 2009 to withdraw the country from ALBA, citing a 'lack of respect' from Venezuela for making remarks about a potential invasion of Honduras to re-establish Manuel Zelaya to office. The relationship between Zelaya and Chávez became one of the main arguments

<2> CMS-Venezuela, 2010: http://www.movimientos. org/show_text. php3?key=17586

among the opposition that he should be overthrown. "The coup leaders want to return to the past to benefit the empire and the oligarchy with the natural resources of our country," stated Rafael Alegría, a leader of the Honduran resistance which has led ongoing street protests since the coup.

Despite ALBA positioning itself as a threat to the neoliberal hegemony, it operates in a regional context in which a full range of leftist and rightist political leaders coexist, and is also inserted in a global capitalist economic model. While only the more 'progressive' governments in the region have directly rejected the neoliberal integration project, others in contrast have signed free trade agreements with the US: Mexico in 1994; Chile in 2002; the Central American countries of Costa Rica, Honduras, Guatemala, Nicaragua, El Salvador and Dominican Republic in 2004 with the CAFTA treaty; and Perú and Colombia in 2006. The EU is also trying to sign free trade agreements with Latin America.

Several contradictions underlie ALBA. Not only with the clear material paradox that its consolidation and growth depends directly on fossil-fuel extraction, as the CMS-Venezuela stated: "As Venezuelans we recognise the big contradiction that we face in this struggle since we are a country supported fundamentally in oil production, knowing that fossil fuels are one of the main causes of climate change. We recognise and support the efforts of the revolutionary government to diversify our economies and to search for more sustainable production ways. Oil has been our fundamental tool in the search for social justice and the peoples' unity, however, we know is not a sustainable way and as united peoples we have to look for other ways to support ourselves towards an endogenous development". But also with the on-growing political influence of Venezuela over the rest of the ALBA members. There are also many instances where the Venezuelan and other ALBA governments continue to use instruments of the state against their populations.

BOLIVIA:

Located at the centre of the South American Andes mountains and stretching to the Amazon in the East, Bolivia is both geographically and culturally very diverse. With two thirds of its inhabitants Indigenous Peoples, Bolivia started rebelling in 1781 when the Indigenous Tupac Katari and Bartolina Sisa led a siege against the Spanish colonisers in La Paz. Katari and Sisa envisioned an interethnic project where indigenous, mestizo, creoles and colonisers could live together. Murdered by the colonial powers, they have become talismans of current indigenous movements.

The decades of 1940s and 50s saw generalised social unrest among workers and peasants, who demanded the abolishment of unpaid and forced labour. Military units were placed along the mountain ranges in response and any attempt of social organisation was violently repressed. However, as the Indigenous saying of those times affirms, "You have arms and airplanes, but we will invade the cities from below". This still prevails in the tactics of current Bolivian movements. Peasants, workers and miners coalesced their demands through the Nationalist Revolutionary Movement (MNR) party and in 1952 attacked the government in La Paz led by the military Hugo Ballivián, giving the presidential seat to the MNR leader Paz Estenssoro. After some minor changes in the constitution, a failed agrarian reform, and attempts to neutralise Indigenous mobilisations, the MNR lost its general popular support. However, several decades later, the miners and workers were still considered a powerful symbol for revolution.

Since a military group overthrew Estenssoro in 1964, successive military *coup d'états* took place until the 80s, creating a period of severe repression and persecution of workers and Indigenous movements. The Bolivian Workers Union (COB) was founded, and in 1979, the CSUTCB *(Confederación Sindical Única de Trabajadores Campesinos de Bolivia)* formed from the merger of several peasant unions. These unions were fundamental in overthrowing the military dictatorships.

In 1985, Paz Estenssoro returned to power, and under the guidance of Gonzalo Sánchez de Lozada started the neoliberal period hand-in-hand with the IMF. Repression was organised now by elected governments instead of the military. In this period, poverty increased enormously, salaries went down and the country was unable to pay its external debt. At the same time, the once strong mining unions that were dominant along with the COB, were weakened as the mines started to be privatised and closed down. Thousands of miners were forced to migrate south, and many became coca growers. Until 1988, there were around 20,800 miners unemployed only from COMIBOL (state-owned mining company) that were forced to migrate with their families. Furthermore, the COB failed to include peasants within its leadership and a series of ruptures within the CSUTCB lasted until early 2000.

The 'war on drugs' financed by the US led to both a cultural clash and an armed conflict over coca leaf production. Coca is seen both as 'dangerous', being the key ingredient in cocaine, which therefore must be eradicated, and at the same time a sacred and traditional plant in Andean cultures. The violent processes of forced coca eradication confronted with popular opposition, meant intense militarisation, tortures and killings of coca growers, especially in the area of Chapare, in the East, where many ex-miners and peasants were left, again, without livelihoods. The coca leaf was transformed into a symbol of resistance against Washington interventions. Over time, the coca growers' movement, led by a young Evo Morales, came to offer the only vibrant national-popular resistance to the dominance of neoliberalism. It was in 1999 that the *'Movimiento al Socialismo'* (MAS) party was created as a 'political tool for the peoples' sovereignty'. MAS generated different dynamics within the Bolivian left by creating a party that is theoretically accountable to social movements as opposed to the traditional left that subsumes everything to party priorities. By developing clear 'anti-imperialist' and 'anti-neoliberal' platforms, MAS established a 'social movement-political party' for the first time in Bolivian history. MAS is therefore both completely unlike other parties yet also striven by tensions between its two identities.

After the harsh neoliberalism of the 1990s, social resistance turned to Cochabamba. The whole city, fuelled by peasants, workers, urban families and coca growers rose up in 2000 and took the streets to prevent the privatisation of water (see box iii). A coalition formed in 1999 called the *'Coordinadora del Agua y la Vida'* or Co-ordinator of Water and Life, was a key organizational instrument for action that brought together peoples from rural areas, urban movements and combined different economic and political sectors. Under the slogan 'The Water is ours, damn it!' the city, airport and main roads were taken over by the peoples with blockades, assemblies for information and discussion, neighbourhood actions, barricades, strikes and constant street occupations. The 'water war', as this struggle would later be known, proved to be the beginning of a radical change in the history of Bolivia.

'The Water is Ours Dammit'- graffiti
on demo 10th anniversary of the
Water Wars, Cochabamba

iii.
THE ONGOING WATER WARS IN BOLIVIA

Occurring just five months after the 'battle of Seattle' mass protests that blockaded the World Trade Organisation (WTO) negotiations, Cochabamba's water war became a key symbol of victory in the struggle against global capitalism. Between January and April 2000 a broad range of movements including workers, farmers, peasants, coca growers, urban families, street children and anarchists took over Cochabamba to successfully de-privatise their water. Hundreds of thousands of people across the country joined into what became a massive showdown with the government involving a general strike, constant road blockades, mass demonstrations and battles with police and army in which five people died.

It all began when the World Bank declared it would not "renew" a $25 million loan to Bolivia unless it privatised its water services. Without regard for its weak bargaining position, the Bolivian government under President Hugo Banzer agreed to the terms of its sole bidder *Aguas del Tunari*, (a multinational consortium including the US-Bechtel) and signed a $2.5 billion, 40-year concession "to provide water and sanitation services to the residents of Cochabamba. The contract granted *Aguas del Tunari* control over the irrigation systems of rural areas and communal water sources, most of which had been constructed and financed by the local inhabitants, as well as increasing water bills by 200%.

An overwhelming majority opposed this, and this opposition led to a more direct cooperation among urban and rural movements. It was also the final straw for people, seeing the neoliberal government privatising anything they could to pay off debts. The *'Coordinadora del Agua y la Vida'* became the core of the diverse resistances that spread across Bolivia. After months of organising, struggle and popular uprising eventually on 9th April the police told the executives of the consortium that their safety could no longer be guaranteed.

The executives then fled from Cochabamba to Santa Cruz. After coming out of four days of hiding, Oscar Olivera, a leader of the factory workers union, signed an accord with the government guaranteeing the removal of Aguas del Tunari and turning Cochabamba's water works over to La Coordinadora. As Olivera reflects later: "The biggest achievement of those days was that we lost our fear... we started to talk among us, to know each other and gain self and collective trust."

In the end water prices in Cochabamba returned to their pre-2000 levels with a group of community leaders running the restored state utility company SEMAPA. However there are ongoing problems. SEMAPA was badly weakened, underfunded and with little prospect of becoming the kind of company that local residents demanded. Since then, access to water has improved and rates have been raised only slightly. However, there is still a long way to go. Half of the 600,000 people of Cochabamba remained without water and those with it only received intermittent service (some as little as three hours a day).

Just days before the CMPCC began, thousands of activists from Bolivia and around the world gathered in Cochabamba to mark the tenth anniversary of the water war as part of the Third International Water Fair. These events were totally independent from the CMPCC. A big demonstration saw banners saying: 'Water is a Right', 'The water is ours, dammit!', and 'Ten Years of Struggle'. We marched from the main square to the factory workers complex. People were arranged in neighbourhoods or districts, and many walked in organised lines. An overwhelming majority were women, many with children and babies. The atmosphere was determined and powerful. One woman explained that in the 'Zona Sur', or Southern Zone of the city, there is still no drinking water and it is expensive for families to buy it. For them the struggle for water is ongoing. Zona Sur has six districts and is home to around 250,000 people, some of the poorest in the city and those most affected by the ineffectiveness of SEMAPA. An additional problem is that the city is expanding rapidly, many coming from Oruro and Potosí due to among other things, the water pollution as a consequence of the constant mining operations in these areas. At the end of the demo there was a platform where water struggles from around the world were represented by the main speakers, giving an overview of the links between water privatisation and how this is a major issue being resisted globally. For example, Francessca Caprini from the Italian Forum talked about how the water in Italy has recently been privatised. The Fair focused on exchanging community strategies for getting the drinking water they need. This included raising money for wells, forming co-operatives, and creating plans for the use of community water. One theme that came out repeatedly was that these current problems will only be exacerbated by climate change. On our final day in Cochabamba we witnessed yet another demo outside the main government offices demanding that they honour a commitment to install water in a neighbourhood of the Zona Sur. 'La Lucha Continúa!' The Struggle Continues.

Just as the 'water war' weakened the legitimacy of traditional political parties and unions, it also strengthened the power and capacity of broad coalitions among a diverse range of social actors and sectors. The indigenous movements were reinvigorated, and started challenging the neoliberal paradigm by demanding redistribution of wealth through the nationalisation of the hydrocarbons: gas and oil.

The so-called 'gas war' came in October 2003 when Sánchez de Lozada (Bolivia's president for the second time during 2002-03) announced the export of Bolivia's gas to Mexico and the US through a Chilean port, a plan made by a corporate consortium composed of British Gas, BP and Repsol/YPF. In response, a diverse mass of peoples took to the streets once again with blockades and mass-protests demanding that the government implement the nationalisation of hydrocarbons. Despite the severe military and police repression, El Alto's neighbourhood assemblies (FEJUVE) mobilised thousands of people in El Alto and La Paz, while Olivera and others mobilised thousands more to the streets in Cochabamba; coca growers in Chapare blocked roads; the miners entered with a massive demo from Oruro to La Paz; the roads to the Peruvian and Chilean borders were blocked; and the COB carried out a general strike that paralyzed the country. The national-popular agenda had been set; nationalisation of gas and no export through Chile. Finally, in 2003 De Lozada was forced to resign.

De Lozada's vice president, Carlos Mesa, assumed power based on his promise to enact the social movements' so-called 'October Agenda' but he also failed to materialise the peoples' demands. In June 2005 new road blockades shut down eight of Bolivia's nine departments with the nation-alisation of hydrocarbons as their central demand. On June 6th, around 400-500,000 protesters, overwhelmingly Ayamaran Indigenous, poured down from El Alto into the heart of La Paz. Carlos Mesa was forced to resign. In December 2005, the MAS party led by Morales won the presidential and legislative elections with an unprecedented 54 percent of the votes, opening a new phase in the political cycle that began with the 'water war'. As the first indigenous president of Bolivia, the Morales government quickly implemented the nationalisation of hydrocarbons and the con-stitutional assembly in order to formulate a new national constitution.

The 'nationalisation' process has not meant in practice a complete and sole public ownership, but rather is a partial form where the state has at least 51% shares in all hydrocarbon interests and an increase on royalties from 50% to 82%. This has allowed the government to create welfare programs that redistribute this wealth to the poorest sectors of society. The constitutional assembly on the other hand started in 2006. After several political conflicts among the right and the left, in 2009 a referendum took take place and with a 61.7% majority, the new constitution came into effect. Its main achievement was to transform Bolivia into a 'Plurinational State', which recognises the diversity of ethnicities and cultures, and Indigenous peoples' rights. Although so far successfully resisted by the government, the elites from the so-called 'Media Luna' (four resource-rich eastern provinces) have threatened progress by attempting to split the country along geological as well as racial lines in a call for regional autonomy. Critics point out that MAS conceded key points to the right in order to be able to govern. For example reforms of land re-distribution are seen as extremely weak.

Using the coca leaf as a political symbol that unites many movements and sectors, and the Wiphala (a multicoloured flag representing the different Indigenous cultures of the Andes) as a symbol for cultural diversity, Morales has mobilised indigenous myths and symbols associated with a radical past. However, as evidenced during the Mesa 18 discussions (see chapter 5), there are several distinct currents amongst indigenous federations and groups, with some demanding that they are not being 'represented' by MAS and that they are still affected by extractive industries and governmental policies.

PEOPLE'S GLOBAL ACTION

The Peoples' Global Action (PGA) network formed as a way for autonomous groups to spread information and coordinate global actions. PGA grew out of the international Zapatista gatherings in 1996 and 1997 and bought together diverse groups united by their opposition to capitalism, and commitment to direct action and civil disobedience as the most effective form of struggle. From the WTO protests in Seattle to the G8 protests in Genoa, many of the groups and movements involved with PGA have been a driving force behind the global anti-capitalist mobilisations. Hundreds of coordinated demonstrations, actions and street parties have taken place on all five continents against intergovernmental meetings promoting free-trade. The network met in international conferences from which the first one (Geneva, 1998) launched a worldwide coordination of resistance against the WTO. The second one was in Bangalore in 1999, and the third one in Cochabamba in 2001.

The basis of unity and political analysis is expressed in the constantly evolving manifesto and hallmarks that involve a clear rejection of capitalism and all forms of domination, and a call for direct action and civil disobedience [3].

<3> Read full texts at www.agp.org

However, Morales represents great hope and inspiration for many Bolivians. Reforms in education, healthcare, raising the minimum wage and doubling job creation have improved the daily lives of Bolivia's poor in ways that many would not have thought possible a few years ago. Coming from the social movements, he is considered by many as 'one of us'. But the push of Morales to incorporate the various indigenous movements into MAS has had its drawbacks. When this started to happen, it left the autonomous movements gutted. For a long time, criticism of the government from the left was hard to come by, because of the immense popularity of MAS and the fear of unwillingly strengthening the anti-government campaign of the right.

Following his re-election in 2009 and five years in government, there is a growing discontent among some movements at the government's failure to go far enough in its reforms, and to turn its radical discourse into practice. Although Morales denounces the evils of capitalism, conversely and to the dismay of many radicals, progressives and victims of the consequences, MAS has financed the reforms by pursuing an export oriented extractivist development model. This model was a major theme at the Third International Water Fair, held just a few days before the climate conference in Cochabamba to commemorate the 'water war' on its ten-year anniversary. This was part of a process to rebuild spaces for discussion, organisation and resistance outside of the government's influence, and from the bottom up.

Although the PGA has undoubtedly acted as inspiration to many groups, the activity of the PGA network seems to have dissipated in recent years. It seems that is partly due to the network's inability to move on from the counter-summit mobilisations that came to define it. The last regional conference was in 2006 but there was a PGA climate caravan to Copenhagen in 2009.

Bolivia was a key part in this global movement of movements as expressed in the reflections from the 3rd PGA International Conference that began less than a week after September 11th, 2001: "The repressive new world order that the USA has justified by the attack in New York was immediately evident... After the attack, the Bolivian government practically sealed the border for PGA and the governor of the province declared to the press that the PGA delegates were all "potential terrorists" and had organised the riots in Europe and North America. The US ambassador publicly threatened Evo Morales, the leader of the Six Federations of the Tropics of Cochabamba, for having dared to simultaneously condemn the terrorist attack and the state terrorism practised by the USA in Iraq, Colombia, etc." This was perhaps influential in Bolivia's ability to mobilise for the CMPCC.

'The Water is Ours'- street in Cochabamba

'Let's be realistic, Demand the impossible',
banner displayed at closing ceremony of CMPCC

3.

WHERE TO BEGIN WITH CLIMATE JUSTICE?

Climate justice is a relatively new term. As a key concept in this text and in our thinking about this project, it is important here to expand upon the different understandings of, and some of the debates surrounding, the term 'climate justice' – though of course no single understanding is right or wrong, and no group can lay claim to a particular concept.

Although it has a much longer history that is difficult to trace, the term was popularised by the formation of the 'Climate Justice Now!' network in Bali during the COP-14 negotiations in 2007. In the build up to the COP-15 in Copenhagen the term became a mobilizing platform across Europe as the 'Climate Justice Action' (CJA) network opposed the COP as an unjust set of negotiations interested in expanding capitalism rather than in addressing the global climate crises.

For many of the groups and networks that participated in CJA the broad position underlying the use of the term is the politicisation of climate change – understanding that it results from our current and historical social relations, and that in order to address it we need fundamental changes to our economic and political systems. The 'injustice' is that the industrialised western world are disproportionately (both historically and currently) responsible for the emissions that are causing climate change, and are now using it as an excuse to accumulate further through the implementation of market-based false solutions. Meanwhile, the geographical and political south will suffer the worst effects of climate change; their territories and resources were plundered and polluted to feed western industrialisation, and now climate change is being used as an excuse to colonise, privatise and dispossess further through the creation of new markets to 'solve' the crisis.

Under the broad banner of climate justice, different groups and networks employ a wide range of tactics – from lobbying and campaigning through to sabotage and direct actions, and everything in between. Many of the struggles are not primarily or explicitly 'climate' struggles but are in fact local struggles against dispossession, exploitation, contamination or industrial expansion in local areas: including those against monoculture plantations in Uganda, hydroelectric dams in Brazil, large-scale wind farms in India, open-cast coal mining in Wales, and exploitation of tar sands in Canada. Others are fighting to prevent the new markets and agreements that will encourage and facilitate more exploitation, accumulation and dispossession – such as opposing and challenging the carbon market, the privatisation of forests or the domination of powerful countries and corporations within international negotiations. The different uses of the term are often (but not always) reflected in the political tactics employed, so for example one understanding of justice may pursue a legal route whereas others reject this and use direct action.

One of the debates around the term is over the extent to which capitalism is identified as the underlying cause of the problem. This debate is exacerbated by conflicting understandings of capitalism itself. How many people have actually considered the values of the economies we live in, what it is that makes them 'capitalist', and what alternatives exist or might look like? There are those, often of a liberal Keynesian persuasion, who have no problem with capitalism per se, only with the neoliberal version of it. They tend to argue that neoliberal policies encourage the worst excesses of capitalism, and that what is preferable is the careful management of capitalism towards the interests of the people. For others, there may for some be a strategical decision to say 'neoliberalism' over 'capitalism' because the former, having clearly definable policies, offers a more tangible enemy than abstract social relations but nonetheless they understand the problem to be capitalism itself, not the way we choose to 'manage' it. Finally, there are those who identify not just a particularly 'pure' form of capitalism as the problem, but capitalist relations themselves – relations based on domination and exploitation in the pursuit of profit. Capitalism, whether mediated by state regulations or otherwise, values profit above all other things.

Another point of contention between different groups are disagreements around discourses of 'climate debt'. These can sometimes come down to an understanding of the word. Understood in a financial sense, climate debt would necessitate the existence of international financial systems within which the debt could be repaid. In a radical climate discourse, there can be no space for such systems.

Understood in a broader sense, climate debt is an attempt to balance severe disequilibrium in emissions produced by the industrialised countries and the consequences experienced by the global south. Reparations in this latter sense are demanded in terms of removal of patents on technologies, so that they are available and free for all. The argument is that climate debt is a political issue, and cannot be reduced to a simple financial transaction that attempts to place a monetary value on the damages done and lives lost as a result of centuries of exploitation. The concept also serves to turn the tables on industrialised nations, to remind people of who has driven the processes of industrialisation – why it is that we're in this mess and how it is that we got here. Given that the demands for reparations are highly unrealistic, the term can often be understood as a tool – like 'climate justice,' it encapsulates many complex issues in one compact phrase.

Similarly, discourses around 'rights' and 'justice' are rejected by many who approach the issue from an anti-authoritarian perspective because they necessitate some authority (in the abstract sense) that has the ability to define what those 'rights' are and what is 'just'. Practically, rights and justice are usually articulated through the legal structures designed by and in service of the state, therefore legitimising and reinforcing oppressive and repressive power structures whose primary function is to protect the property rights necessary for capitalism to flourish. Where such legal structures do not yet exist (as, for example, in many indigenous communities), their establishment serves to force incorporation into the established hegemonic system of commodification and exchange.

However, others consider that the use of courts and binding regulations in the form of 'laws' and 'rights' can be instrumental for holding corporations accountable for their innumerable local crimes. In parts of what developed into the 'Environmental Justice' movement, frontline communi-

'Enough Racism' from Mujeres Creando social centre, La Paz

ties of colour in the US used the existing legal structures and the language of rights to successfully resist structural environmental racism and industrial dumping in their neighbourhoods.

Altogether outside of this spectrum lie organizations and coalitions such as TckTckTck, who have begun to co-opt the term. TckTckTck's 'join the fight for climate justice' campaign offers no definition of climate justice, but plenty of guilt-and-pity evoking prose and photos bemoaning the disastrous consequences of climate change without ever alluding to the possible, political, causes. The campaign calls on politicians to agree to 'fair, ambitious and binding emissions cuts' – reinforcing a concept of justice and a method of attaining it that encourages faith in the systems and power relations responsible for the situation in the first place. Given that the Climate Justice Now! network was formed partly as a response from the smaller or more radical NGOs to the un-acceptable pro-carbon market, pro-techno-fix positions of the bigger NGOs in the Climate Action Network, the appropriation of this term is yet another attempt to recuperate a radical concept.

It is obvious that the term 'climate justice' as yet lacks a single clear definition and is used by different groups in different ways. However, most share a common basic analysis of the historical responsibility, distribution of consequences and rejection of market solutions that make climate change a political, rather than a technical, issue.

29

March through Cochabamba to the 3rd International Water Fair

4.

PRODUCING THE PEOPLES' AGREEMENT

According to the Bolivian government, the CMPCC brought together more than 35,000 participants from 142 countries, with almost 10,000 visiting Bolivia from abroad. There were government representatives present from 48 countries. The overwhelming participation came from within Latin America, followed by a substantial number from North America. Europe and Asia were poorly

PROCESS OF THE CMPCC

represented – both relied on flights through Europe, which were largely disrupted by the erupting Icelandic volcano. Representation from Africa was also low: whilst the volcano may have had some impact, the cost of reaching Bolivia from much of the continent excluded the vast majority of potential participants.

The conference process began more than a month before the physical event itself; seventeen working groups were created around a series of topics ranging from climate debt to food sovereignty to the structural causes of the climate crisis. Each of these working groups had an open email list which, in theory, would be used to produce an initial document to be presented at the beginning of the conference. Whilst this online process deserves merit for its attempt to include those who could not attend, from our experience the process was ineffective. Whilst people sent reports and position papers, there was very little analysis or debate and the lack of translation was also an obstacle. The work on these lists was then synthesised by a government appointed 'moderator' into the initial working group text.

Parallel to this there was also a pre-conference where around 500 representatives from six grassroots organisations of Bolivia gathered in Cochabamba on 29th and 30th March to discuss the Bolivian position on the topics of the different working groups. This pre-conference also involved several ministerial representatives and the president, Evo Morales. The result was seventeen documents which were presented to the respective CMPCC working groups, and the meeting initiated the start of local discussions around the summit.

With the online process lacking in real debates, and suspicions about the initial government appointed moderators, many participants feared that the process was being 'cooked' by the Bolivian government. For example, in the forests working group the moderator presented an initial document that supported the REDD mechanism (Reduced Emissions through Deforestation and Degradation) – despite there also being documents opposing this – reflecting the

position of the Bolivian government as one of the global flagships for REDD schemes. There was certainly much confusion as a result of the online process.

At the conference, each of the working groups began with the same mandate – to take the document prepared on the email lists and, through a process of open debate over two and a half days, develop a more expanded and comprehensive document. In practice each group operated differently, to greater or lesser effect, in producing their document. The first task was to elect two secretaries and two chairs, whose role was to document and facilitate the discussions respectively. In both cases it was required that there was a male and a female, and a national and an international, in each role. In some cases this was done immediately, whilst others left it to the end of the first day so as to gain familiarity with those they were working with.

Some groups rejected the initial documents out of hand and set about creating a new text from scratch. Whilst, for example, the 'action strategies' group left their document largely intact, the forests working group went through a process, at many times conflictual, of information sharing, heated discussions and consensus building, most notably concerning the controversial topic of REDD. Notwithstanding the differing methodologies, not all of which can be accounted for here, each working group produced a final document which was then submitted to a closed meeting. These meetings, comprising of the secretaries, chairs, the moderator of each group and government officials, were tasked with 'trimming' each document down to four pages for presentation the following day.[4]

These documents, organised into sets of three, were then orated by the working group chairs to sports halls and basketball courts packed full of participants. As each was read out, a queue formed of people who had comments or had not had a chance to contribute, and one by one additions were suggested or statements rejected. Perhaps one of the most important moments in these final stages occurred in the 'action strategies' session, during which *Via Campesina* and

<4> The full text of each working group can be found on the official summit website: http://pwccc. wordpress.com/category/working-groups/

the landless peasant movement, the MST, made a formal submission for all references to a top-down initiative of organising movements to be taken out from the final declaration. Finally, each of the amended texts were then taken to another closed meeting, in which the final 'Peoples' Agreement' was produced. To what extent these interventions were taken on board is questionable; for example the final text still maintained a less explicit reference to a 'top-down' organisation of movements. However, most of the working group decisions were maintained in the final document.

PLENARIES AND WORKSHOPS

Running alongside and complimentary to the Peoples' Agreement process were 14 plenaries and more than 160 'self-organised' workshops.

The plenaries informed the working group discussions and included famous figures such as Vandana Shiva, Naomi Klein and Jim Hansen, as well as government representatives like the Bolivian vice president, Alvaro Garcia Linera. This was a very important part of producing the documents and a chance to learn more about the issues. It was physically impossible to attend them all, but in many cases working groups were in effect suspended as participants attended the relevant plenaries.[5] The self-organised workshops also contributed to the debates in the working groups, but were even more broad-ranging, including topics such as water resources and eco-socialism. Some were official representatives presenting cases from their countries, while others, like ours, looked to contribute to the collective creation of strategies outside of the formal processes (see box vi).

It was a very crammed programme and tough choices had to be made about what to attend. This reduced opportunities for the cross-fertilisation of ideas as working group time already felt pressured and often clashed with self-organised events and plenaries.

<5> A full list of the plenaries and workshops can be found here: http://www.ifg.org/pdf/program-cmcc-english-final-v-2.pdf

'Without water there is no beer!' a banner on Water War demo, Cochabamba

SIN AGUA NO'HAY CHICHA

5.

It is clear that the politics of Bolivia are constantly changing and contested. This was key to the most notable of the meetings that took place outside the conference, called the Mesa 18, or 18th table, so named as there were 17 official working groups in the CMPCC. Following a pre-conference organised by CONAMAQ, a national indigenous council, it was set up by groups wanting to highlight the contradictions between the Bolivian government's external discourses on capitalism and the rights of Mother Earth, and its ongoing support for domestic megaprojects and reliance on extractive industries.

CONFRONTING CONTRADICTIONS

MESA 18

As Carlos Crespo Flores, one of the organisers, put it:

"What we saw again in Copenhagen is that externally our president is the defender of the mother earth, of nature, but internally he is doing the opposite- we have seen this, this is our experience. And then we realised that they were trying to hide these internal contradictions, and we thought, why don't we do an event, a table, where we make these visible, these internal themes, the contradictions of our president?"

The Bolivian government reacted strongly, publicly condemning the 18th Mesa and making accusations that it received funding from right wing politicians. These allegations played on the sensitive situation in Bolivia regarding criticism of the government. Many feel that dissenting voices from the social movements that brought Morales to power are kept in check by the fear of fuelling right wing opposition, losing the progress made in terms of indigenous representation and collective self-esteem, and a possible return to darker times under previous governments. The 18th Mesa responded to this dilemma by positioning itself as a parallel process, rather than a counter summit. Despite this cautious but critical approach, there was an attempt by two right wing MPs to capitalise on any divisions by trying to participate in the Mesa. However, they were met with fiercely vocal opposition and were very publicly forced to leave the discussions.

As with the CMPCC itself, the 18th Mesa had complications with its democratic processes (a reminder that no process is infallible!) During the initial stages some NGOs attempted to draft the text behind closed doors, and asked CONAMAQ to present it, emulating the way in which governments and institutions attempt to give legitimacy to their positions by co-opting indigenous voices. This raised serious discontent and threatened to de-rail the process. However, in the end a statement was produced with broad involvement from those participating. It strongly rejects neoliberal development, extractivism and trans-nationals, and is highly critical of the NGOs and governments that support them. At the same time it promotes collective rights, the rights of Mother Earth and communal control of natural resources.

STRUGGLES AGAINST EXTRACTION

Throughout the period of the climate summit, 500km from Cochabamba in Potosí, local communities took action against the San Cristóbal Mining Company, currently owned by the Japanese Sumitomo Corporation, which is the world's third largest producer of silver and sixth largest of zinc. Frustrated by the extraction of natural resources and contamination of the community's water, people blockaded the company, occupied its offices and started overturning trains full of mineral ore close to the Chilean border- a real example of the struggle against extractive industries. The struggles in San Cristóbal was instrumental in showing that words were not enough and that action is needed.

Along with the mining in San Cristóbal, which was also denounced during the mesa 18, around 300 Ween-hayek, Tapiete and Guaraníes indigenous from the Gran Chaco area carried out a demonstration against the Morales government who authorised oil operations in their territories, violating their constitutional right of previous consultation.

The struggles continue...

"To challenge climate change humanity needs to remember its cultural collective communitarian roots – this means building a society based on collective property and in the communal and rational management of natural resources, where the peoples decide in a direct way the destiny of natural wealth in accordance with their organising structures, their self determination, their norms and procedures and their vision of how to manage their territories. History teaches us that there is only one effective way to transform society and to construct a social alternative to capitalism, that is the permanent mobilisation and articulation of our struggles."[6]

Mesa 18 was an example of pushing the boundaries of debate and was an invaluable part of the process. There are plans to continue networking so that those struggles that are normally quite separate have an ongoing opportunity to communicate.

The need for this kind of opposition becomes clear when we consider the Initiative for the Integration of Regional Infrastructure in South America (IIRSA). It was presented and accepted in 2000 during the meeting of Presidents of South America in Brasilia, Brazil, "To promote the development of transport, energy and

IIRSA communications infrastructure from a regional viewpoint, aimed at the physical integration of the twelve South American countries and the achievement of an equitable and sustainable territorial development pattern." However, in reality, this enormous initiative is threatening vast territories and having severe impacts on the livelihoods of local communities. At the same time it is accelerating resource extraction and intensifying the neoliberal model of economic growth.

<6> CMS-Venezuela, 2010: http://www.movimientos.org/show_text.php3?key=17586

IIRSA is currently in the implementation phase and includes a series of large-scale and debt-heavy mega-projects that result in direct and indirect impacts on biodiversity conservation, small farms, agricultural practices, local territories and livelihoods of Indigenous peoples and other traditional communities. Illegal logging along new roads and waterways will also impact extensive areas of the Amazon region. Such projects are displacing communities, increasing deforestation and forcing people to migrate. The roads and ports are mainly intended to stimulate exports of primary materials such as soya beans, timber and minerals. The underlying assumption is that trade liberalization and regional insertion into global markets will lead to sustainable development, and therefore mountains, forests, and local communities are perceived as 'barriers' to economic growth, while rivers are used as infra-structure for extracting other natural resources.

This 'regional integration' model is ruled by a Directive Executive Committee, with representatives from each of the twelve countries, and a Committee of Technical and Financial Coordination, with representatives from three multilateral financial organizations: the Inter-American Development Bank (IDB), the Andean Finance Corporation (CAF) and the Financial Fund for the Development of the River Plate Basin (FONPLATA). With financing for projects reaching 70 billion USD, this initiative is significantly increasing the region's external debt. Moreover, IIRSA also consists of several pro-cesses of legal integration designed to harmonise regulatory frameworks between countries.

Graffiti Cochabamba

May Day demo - La Paz

One IIRSA project is the construction of the Inambari hydroelectric dam in the Peruvian Amazon. This will be the 5th largest dam in South America and most of the energy generated will be purchased by Brazil. This construction is expected to flood 45 thousand hectares of forests and to impact on the National Park Bahuaja Sonene, home of Indigenous communities and rich biodiversity. The Indigenous Federation of Madre de Dios is trying to resist this project warning that it will force entire communities to migrate. In March 2010 massive mobilizations made a 48 hour road block in Puno preventing any access to the city, the university was taken by students and the municipal office was attacked, with the central demand of stopping Inambari and releasing the imprisoned community leaders. Although construction is still ongoing, local resistance is continuing to delay the planned completion of the project.

In spite of being based on principles that are in direct opposition to the ALBA integration model (see box ii), both Bolivia and Venezuela are part of IIRSA as well. This evidences the fundamental contradictions between rhetoric and practice of the Bolivarian project and thus became a main focus during the Mesa 18 discussions, which as the first conclusion of their declaration stated: "We renounce imperialism, transnationals and the so called progressive Latin American governments that implement mega energy and infrastructure projects under the IIRSA in any of Latin American territories – particularly in indigenous territories and protected areas – which are designed by banks, businessmen and private builders with a neoliberal and exploitative vision."

UNASUR   Another form of regional integration was created in 2004, parallel to the creation of ALBA, when the twelve South American countries decided to form the South American Nations Community (Comunidad Sudamericana de Naciones – CSN), which was later changed to the South American Nations Union (Unión Sudamericana de Naciones – UNASUR). This initiative has the main objectives of promoting competition through joint infrastructure projects and promoting convergence between the two commercial blocks: CAN (Perú, Ecuador, Colombia and Bolivia) and MERCOSUR (Argentina, Brazil, Uruguay, Paraguay and Venezuela). The IIRSA initiative has been included under the UNASUR umbrella.

"There are still contradictions found in the integration agreements such as MERCOSUR, ALBA, etc. There is a critique of capitalism but we are still dominated by foreign transnationals, and we are still talking within capitalist terms because they follow the same development paradigm. Moreover, the power alliances are heterogeneous which compromises us onto capitalist policies promoted by the elites that run some of the countries in the region."[7]

<7> Full transcription in English and Spanish available here: http://cochabamba2010. typepad.com/blog/2010/05/mesa-18-declaration-english-spanish.html

May Day demo - La Paz

6.

WHAT WE DID IN BOLIVIA

Once we had decided to attend the conference the work began to prepare, organise events, consider feedback and get in touch with interesting people and movements that would be there. Our time in Bolivia was divided between three main areas: Distributing the Open Letter, attending workshops, plenaries and side-events, and participating in events happening outside of the conference.

Not being representatives of any group or movement, we as individuals wanted to pull together some common perspectives that we could discuss with people we met in Bolivia. To this end we wrote and distributed thousands of copies of an open letter, which had the backing of the Amsterdam meeting of CJA (see box

THE OPEN LETTER

vi). We used this as a base for the interviews that we did, networking, informal discussions and our workshop – Building Bridges Across Continents with Grassroots Climate Justice Movements (see box vi).

The groups that we participated in were action strategies, migration, forests and structural causes. The working groups were quite intense and exciting to take part in, with each comprising of around a hundred or more people crammed into a university seminar room. At times passions ran high with people getting up onto tables to yell across at each other, but there was also a genuine desire amongst participants to listen and share ideas.

WORKING GROUPS

Here we feedback from two groups to give a flavour of what happened.

MIGRATION IS NOT A CRIME!

"As workers migrate from south to north, new models of unequal exchange are created in which migration acts as another transfer to the north." Raul Delgado Wise

Unlike the COP process, the Bolivian government was keen to consider the social impacts of climate change, including recognition and protections for those directly affected. Increasingly people are being forced to leave their homes due to the effects of climate change, and like other migrants they are criminalised. As people involved in migration politics in Europe, participating in the Climate Migrants working group was one of the main motivations for attending the conference.

The group talked extensively about terminology – forced migrant, climate refugee, climate displaced – reflecting this

WHAT IS CLIMATE JUSTICE ACTION (CJA)?

Climate Justice Action is a network that formed during the mobilisations in the run up to COP-15. Taking a broadly anti-capitalist stance, it positioned itself against the false and market-based solutions being promoted in the UNFCCC, and calls for fundamental changes to the economic and political systems that are the root cause of the climate crisis. The process of forming the network began in September 2008 when a meeting was held in Copenhagen, just prior to the European Social Forum, to discuss the summit and how to mobilise around it. Initial discussions centred around the legitimacy of the summit, with the 'shut them down or shut them in' debate reflecting a complex diversity of opinions. Attitudes towards a UN climate summit were not as simple as in previous summit mobilisations, with some fearing that without the UN there was no alternative forum for making urgently needed emissions cuts, whilst others taking firmly antagonistic attitudes towards what they considered to be nothing more than a mechanism for the expansion of ('green') capitalism.

As these debates continued, international mobilisation meetings continued to be held, during which a decision was made to organise mass actions opposing the summit. The concept of the 'Reclaim Power' action was the coming together of the diverse groups and networks involved, and was based around combining an inside and outside strategy, where those outside would attempt to enter the UN area to reclaim the people's power, whilst those inside would disrupt the sessions and meet the other group outside to hold a People's Assembly. The Bolivian delegates played a role here in articulating radical critiques from the inside, often going much further than many of the European climate activists who remained scared off from using the 'big C' word.

In the event the two groups were unable to meet, and the People's Assembly happened outside the conference centre fence. There are many different reflections and evaluations of why the action didn't happen as planned, and there are lessons to be learnt. But the real measures of success are to be found in the wider political impacts, rather than whether or not police lines were crossed.

As well as joining with Climate Justice Now! to organise the Reclaim Power mass action, Climate Justice Action acted as a platform for groups organising other mass actions during the summit targeting a range of issues including migration, agriculture, and production. Since Copenhagen the network has continued to meet. Although now mainly with groups based in Europe, the network continues to have input from participants in other parts of the world.

CJA is currently mobilising for the 12 October Global Day of Action for Climate Justice (see box xi) as a relatively new area of work, and resulting from deeper political questions about categorising human beings and what frameworks and demands are appropriate. The category 'climate refugee' is problematic as it illegitimately constructs and privileges one 'type' of migrant – 'ecological' – over others – 'economic'. Apart from the difficulty of proving that a person or entire community has been displaced by climate change, research shows that migrants are forced by a complex mixture of political, ecological and economic factors. Who can say definitively what role deforestation, poverty, or a trade agreement had alongside climatic changes? Would it include those displaced by extractive industries or false solutions such as bio-fuel plantations?

Discussing categorisation is fundamentally important in the current context of immigration debates in Europe, that are dominated by right-wing and racist voices. Many fear that opening up the category of refugee to include those displaced by environmental factors could risk losing altogether the limited protection offered by international refugee laws.

As a country with a high level of outward migration and internal displacement, rural to urban, the Bolivian perspective in the working group was very important. People spoke of the fact that climate related displacement and associated migration is not a new thing, especially in Bolivia. During the early 1980s there were a series of droughts that forced many Quechua people from the Potosí region into the cities. What was spoken of was the need to make these displacements visible. Participants from across Latin America talked about the short and long term impacts of extreme weather events, mudslides, droughts etc. From a European perspective we were able to talk a little more about the overall context of the repressive migration policies that we see, and the impacts that they have. The final declaration of the conference urged "global north" countries to eliminate their restrictive immigration policies, welcome those forced to migrate by climate change and recognise their fundamental rights.

We distributed a text, "Freedom of Movement in an age of climate chaos", [8] ran a workshop and spoke on a panel arguing that freeedom to stay and freedom of movement for all must become a fundamental part of calls for climate justice. Workshop participants shared the belief that we are one human race made up of many cultures, and that borders are imposed on us for the benefit of capital. While capital enjoys free movement, meaning resources from the south flow to become riches in the north, people are prevented from following these resources and face displacement due to industrial and capitalist practices. [9]

We discussed how it isn't coincidental that the migration policies of differing countries are so similar, coming from a broader policy of global managed migration which is promoted and administered by the International Organisation for Migration (IOM). Their involvement within the working group was of concern to many participants, who articulated different examples of their anti-migrant practices and policies. While they remained within the working group, they did not make proposals towards the final text, and by their presence instigated vital discussions amongst those working in solidarity with migrants around the world.

[8] http://ayya2cochabamba.wordpress.com/ texts-and-articles/border-controls-and-freedom-of-movement-in-an-age-of-climate-chaos/

[9] For more information, articles and feedback see ayya2cochabamba.wordpress.com

While the UN climate negotiations are discussing how (and not if) the carbon dioxide absorbed by forests can be privatised and traded within the carbon market, the forests working group at the Peoples' Summit in Cochabamba joined the opposition voices by firmly rejecting these false solutions. But it was not easy. Two and a half days of heated discussion around a very controversial UN scheme known as REDD (Reducing Emissions from Deforestation and Degradation) built up inspiring and difficult discussions over issues such as self-identity, the definition of 'pueblos' and the real threats to forests. In the end, the working group stated in general consensus: "We condemn neoliberal market mechanisms such as the REDD mechanism and its + and ++ versions, which are violating our Peoples' sovereignty and right to free, prior and informed consent; as well as the sovereignty of national states. This mechanism is violating the rights, uses, and customs of the Peoples and the Rights of Nature."

FORESTS ARE NOT FOR SALE!

"REDD is branded as a friendly forest conservation program, yet it is backed by big polluters. REDD is a dangerous distraction from the root issue of fossil fuel pollution, and could mean disaster for forest-dependent Indigenous Peoples the world over" Alberto Saldamando, legal counsel for the International Indian Treaty Council

vii. ## 'BUILDING BRIDGES ACROSS CONTINENTS WITH GRASSROOTS CLIMATE JUSTICE MOVEMENTS' WORKSHOP

We used this space to introduce the movements within Europe, their politics and a bit of background on the mobilisation for Copenhagen through Climate Justice Action. We had a good turn out, with a variety of people from different struggles and different parts of the world. We know this as we asked everyone to give some details of where they came from and the struggles they are involved in, and then visualised this on an upside-down map.

After inviting a few participants to explain a bit more about the work they were involved with, we split into groups to discuss the question of 'who are our allies and what are the obstacles in building climate justice?' These discussions went for about 45 minutes and then we spent the rest of the time planning for the day of action on Oct 12th (see box xi).

Despite our concerns about using a format that may have been unfamiliar to some, the feedback we received was that in fact people appreciated the face to face interaction and the opportunity to express themselves which was lacking in other workshops. There were lots of ideas for the October 12th day of action, such as being inclusive enough so that different tactics can be used by different groups, and coordinating some of the media work so that actions are not isolated.

At the end of the workshop many people exchanged contact details and hopefully some groundwork was done in getting people talking back in their local networks.

The REDD scheme assumes that deforestation happens because there is no economic value placed on intact forests, and that providing money for conservation to forested countries in the south will help to protect them. However, as the statement from the Durban Group for Climate Justice affirms: "REDD's focus on the mass production of pollution licenses for industries in rich countries would inevitably neglect the needs and violate the rights of ordinary people throughout the world. In the south, REDD would transform the carbon in living trees into private property so that it can be awarded or transferred to private corporations in the north. In the worst case, REDD could inaugurate a massive land grab that would leave Indigenous Peoples and forest-dependent communities with nothing. In the north, meanwhile, REDD credits would enable fossil fuel-related corporations to maintain business as usual, to the detriment of communities affected by fossil fuel extraction and pollution."[10]

> Marlon Santi, President of CONAIE, the Confederation of Indigenous Nationalities of Ecuador, who participated in the forests working group said "REDD has been created by multilateral institutions like the World Bank that routinely violate Indigenous Peoples' rights and pollute Mother Earth. It is perverse that these institutions are pretending to have the 'solution' when they have actually caused the climate crisis. REDD should not be implemented in any country or community."

In this sense, the classroom filled with campesinos, Indigenous Peoples, students, activists, urban groups, among others, condemned the UN definition of forests, saying that "the definition used in the negotiations of the UNFCCC, which includes plantations, is unacceptable. Monoculture plantations are not forests. Therefore, we require a definition for negotiation purposes that recognises the native forests, jungles and the diverse ecosystems on Earth."

The real drivers of deforestation, which is a discussion completely absent within the UN negotiations, were repeatedly highlighted during the discussions, stating in the final document, "Deforestation and forest degradation are the outcome of a historical process of colonial exploitation, of the capitalist system, and of over-consuming developed countries". Besides interesting and enriching discussions among peoples from different parts of the world and sectors of societies, the process of reaching consensus while dealing with such difficult and delicate issues made us aware that we have much more common grounds than we usually believe. Something we accomplished besides the document was the formation of informal anti-REDD networks and the collective understanding among the peoples involved in these discussions of how much a threat REDD can be and how many layers it has.[11] Bolivia currently hosts one of the largest REDD pilot projects and it is yet to be seen if the Morales government will comply with the decisions the peoples made in Cochabamba.

[10] www.durbanclimatejustice.org

[11] http://pwccc.wordpress.com/2010/04/29/final-conclusions-working-group-14-forests/

OUTSIDE THE CONFERENCE.

As we said before, we did not go to Bolivia as delegates of any group or movement, which raised some interesting questions itself about representation, but equally we did not attend for personal interest alone. We also wrote and researched for blogs, articles and this booklet. There was very little mainstream coverage of the conference and so trying to communicate back to our local groups and networks was a key part of our work. We took part in many other events to give us a slightly broader understanding of the Bolivian context. This began with the Third Water Fair, which celebrated 10 years since the water war (see box iii). We met with local active groups and organisers including youth radical groups, anti-REDD groups, and movements networks such as Climate Justice Now! and Rising Tide. We also spoke on a friend's local radio show, 'Rebelde', and a communal radio, CEPJA.

In the main square of Cochabamba, Red Tinku[12], a local activist group, co-ordinated a permanent space of collective learning and reflection. There are people there everyday, using popular education to talk together about issues going on- the water wars, the climate summit, the new anti-corruption laws, local environmental issues such as water, pollution, etc. Red Tinku also run regular tours of the alternative, political history of the city. This visited key houses of the colonial period, monuments to the resistance, the local prison and the *campesino's* (peasant farmer) union building.

Immediately after the summit we were invited to attend the national congress of the CSUTCB. The different regional organisations came together to chose a new president and leaders for the next 5 years. The location of this in Sucre, the country's official capital, was of great political significance. Just a few years ago a racist, right wing mob publicly humiliated and beat indigenous Evo supporters in the main city square. The march through the city was tense but was also an attempt to reclaim their right to be there and was a powerful reminder of how racialised Bolivia remains. Evo Morales spoke at the opening of the conference. It was an interesting opportunity to see him with his base of support, calling for unity and warning against division within the movement. Many people were there specifically as accountable representatives and it as a noticeable difference that we were largely there as individuals.

Our final trip was accompanying the May Day marches in La Paz, where we saw the demands of the unions and the workers pressurising Evo for a higher increase to the basic wage, from 5% to 12%. As we were leaving a national strike was beginning. "Its not against Evo...despite the scale of the strikes etc., we haven't arrived at any sort of crisis. The union sector is completely co-opted by the government. They have bought headquarters, the money comes from Chávez, they have used these methods to control the union movement." (Carlos Crespo Flores)   <12> www.redtinku.com

viii.

AN IMMIGRATION RAID

"Open the door. Police. Immigration. Open the door." are the shouts from along the corridor, and the heavy footsteps come closer and closer. Room by room is visited by the scores of police, flanked by members of the local immigration squad. We are each required to find our passports while answering questions as to our identities, countries of origin, place of arrival and reasons for being in Bolivia. The more unlucky in our group are subjected to full room and bag searches, as the raised voices and loud banging on doors continue around the building. We each had our different conversations with the authorities in our individual rooms, and are led to believe that we're on the receiving end of an immigration raid, linked to the upcoming conference, and as part of a strategy to ensure that there are no 'undesirables' in town as politicians and heads of state begin to arrive.

Later in the day we were told, with amusement, of a news piece that had been seen on a local television channel. A policemen inspects rooms in a local hostel, holding up slightly ripped bedsheets to camera, and pointing out signs of damp on the walls. He proudly explained the authorities role in ensuring that standards and conditions are good enough for the impending influx of foreigners heading to take part in the conference. While that might explain the continuing and vast amount of improvements that have been made to our hostel since our arrival, none of us recollect any of our early morning uninvited guests paying much attention to the state of our walls or our beds.

Other work done in the area in the run up to conference was the covering of the saw mill outside the conference site, the banning of alcohol in the area and rise in prices in all hotels to force migrant workers out of hostel places for the duration of the conference.

7.

QUESTIONS FROM A MOVEMENT

As described in the introduction, as people who identify as critical anti-capitalists and anti-authoritarians
attending a state-sponsored conference, our attend-
ance was not unproblematic. We participated asking
ourselves a number of questions and engaging in many
discussions, not only about the conference itself and its political role, but also with the participants
who attended. Prior to the conference we co-produced and distributed the 'open letter' (see box i),
signed by CJA Amsterdam meeting, addressed to all participants in the conference. At the end of this
letter we posed four questions:

- Do you think that the UNFCCC and the COP process can be effectively used to bring
  about climate justice? If so, how?

- What are the possibilities and dangers of social movements cooperating with
  governments and the state?

- Is climate justice possible without moving beyond capitalist relations?

- What does solidarity mean, and how can we work together more effectively to build
  the transnational struggle for climate justice? What are your views on the 'global
  south' and 'global north' and their relationships to struggle?

These questions were intended to be provocative; we wanted to problematise the conference
itself and the messy relations between movements and states, to directly confront the
assumption that the UNFCCC was a legitimate or effective institution, and to contribute to the
development of responses that aim for systemic transformations to address climate change.
Additionally, and perhaps most importantly, we wanted to begin a collective exploration of the
politics of solidarity, what it means to be 'in solidarity' with others, and how we can act more
effectively in solidarity across international and class divides.

Over the course of the three weeks or so that we were in Bolivia we conducted a series of interviews, ranging from participants in the 'formal' conference process to the organisers of the Mesa 18,
'Cochabambino' feminists, and activists preparing to confront the COP16 in Mexico. To be clear – the
interviews do not represent the diverse range of political approaches present at the conference. We
were not, and are not, interested in presenting world-views we fundamentally disagree with – that is
not the purpose of this booklet. Rather, we looked for those voices that offered a different perspective, different ways for us to think about and understand the questions that we were asking.

What follows is a presentation of the responses to the questions we asked, considering the similarities and divergences between them and discussing the interesting points which they raised for us. Furthermore, the responses we received led us to present a further question exploring the meaning of 'climate justice' – we deemed this question a prerequisite to understanding the further questions, and have consequently termed it 'Question Zero'.

A full list of those we interviewed, along with short biographies and how we came into contact with them, can be found at the end of this book.

'Climate Justice' is a concept that was so central to the COP-15 mobilisations that by the time we came to write the Open Letter (see Box i.), we didn't think it necessary to ask directly what it meant. However, we

7A. WHOSE CLIMATE JUSTICE?

soon realised that its definition was central to the other questions and so we began to include it in our interviews- it became our question zero.

While some of the people we spoke to were unfamiliar with the term its meaning seemed quite clear. For example Marcela Olivera told us, "I haven't really thought about this but I think what we are trying to say when we talk about climate justice is that we all share responsibilities about something that's happening right now. That's also not in an equal way but more in who is causing this and who are the ones that should be accountable for what's happening to all of us."

Beyond this, and reflecting some of the debates in Europe about its relevance to building a radical movement, it became clear to us that the meaning of climate justice is contested in how it should be used as a framework for action. This lack of a clear common understanding leaves the term open to (mis)interpretation and recuperation (see section 3).

At its base the reason that the term is so ripe for co-optation comes down to the very different interpretations of what 'justice' can mean. Christian Guerrero said, "We have to be cautious about definitions. There are already examples of how the UN and governments have manipulated these terms and used them to their advantage. We, not we as the global south, but we as the struggle from below, need to think about how we are going to use and define these terms".

While agreeing that climate justice was needed, Mayeli Sánchez expressed scepticism about the use of what she saw as a westernised version of the concept. Carlos Crespo Flores said that while the idea of climate justice had previously been powerful and come from a radical discourse it was now being used by the Bolivian government in its calls for reparations for climate debt and an international court for climate justice. He warned that principles of private property often lie behind such discourses of rights and justice and explained the case of the right to water as being illustrative here in having generated conflicts (see box x).

But it is not only the state that uses a rights-based approach, many other civil society groups do as well. Whilst they may do so with good intentions, this can end up supporting the establishment of western conceptions of 'property'. As the water example shows, even when rights are conceived of as collective, common resources end up being commodified. Community relations can then become pressured when money is offered in exchange for the these newly created rights. This can be seen in many instances of carbon trading or REDD projects.

For example, early in 2010, the indigenous Ogiek people from the Mau forests in Kenya were displaced from their territories by a UN funded REDD-type project.[13] For the UN, the companies that were awarded the 'rights' to this land are "helping the land managers in the Mau forest area to set up a carbon project. They will undertake to plant native trees on deforested and degraded areas of the forest".[14] By placing 'rights' on these territories, the government created a commodity that can be traded in a way that ignores the livelihoods of those who live there. "The Ogiek community are not going to move out of this forest for one reason: these are our ancestral homes" said Jospeh K. Sang, a representative of the Ogiek community. But since the rights were created and awarded to various companies, the Ogiek people have had no choice.

But the contentions were not limited to the imposition of western concepts of property. Severino Sharupe told us that, "When we speak about justice we speak about healing something. It's a matter of coming together, changing our thinking, it's a brother/sister hood. Maybe you understand justice as penalisation or punishment and that for us means wars, fights and separation." This highlighted questions around the concept of retributive justice (punishment), particularly interesting in light of the People's Accord's call for the establishment of an International Court of Climate and Environmental Justice.

To the extent that Climate Tribunals have been used in the past, they have often been employed as tools for public engagement and discussion or as platforms for affected communities to denounce the criminals, for example at the KlimaForum during COP-15. Trade struggles have also used 'Peoples Tribunals' as a tool to highlight corporate global injustices and to offer affected communities a platform for denouncing corporations' local crimes. The mechanism of a court can have the practical effect of exposing the absurdity of global power imbalances and inequalities, and highlighting the inadequacies and biases inherent to international legal frameworks. Relying upon a subjective definition of justice and an arbitrary power to implement that definition, these legal systems largely serve the interests of the most powerful global actors and reinforce existing global power relations. Severino's comment raised questions around whether the concept of retributive justice, common to western legal systems, makes any sense if the aim is to create a more 'just' future for everyone? Given current global power-relations any real desire for retribution is certainly unrealistic.

Finally, Colin Rajah warned us that "the political construction of the global north-global south is playing out even within the movements that we have, in the sense that organisations and movements in the US and Europe kind of direct and move a lot of where things are going for example within the climate justice movement." He explained that while there were historical connections with the environmental justice movement, whereas that movement had grown from front-line community struggles across the US, the term 'climate justice' had not developed in the same way. This doesn't necessarily mean that climate justice is not useful as a term, but does serve as an extra reminder to be careful how we use it.

<13> Robyn Dixon, Jan 04 2010, "Kenyan tribe slowly driven off its ancestral lands"www. articles.latimes.com/keyword/mwai-kibaki

<14> Chris Lang, Nov 2009, "Ogiek threatened with eviction from Mau Forest, Kenya", REDD-monitor: http://www.redd-monitor. org/2009/11/19/ogiek-threatened-with-eviction-from-mau-forest-kenya/

Maybe the only real justice is what can be gained by the exercise of collective action, against the threats that capitalism and climate change pose to all of our lives, and for the creation of other forms of life outside of capitalism. In this vein, instead of worrying about conflicting definitions, maybe we should listen to the advice that Leonardo Cerdo gave us; "It doesn't matter what we call it; what matters is how we take action."

7B. THE UNITED NATIONS FRAMEWORK CONVENTION ON CLIMATE CHANGE – TOOL FOR CHANGE?

Do you think that the UNFCC and the COP process can be effectively used to bring about climate justice? If so, how?

Debates continue about the legitimacy of the UN as an institution and its ability to solve the climate crises. While it is supposed to be a space for governments to reach an agreement, few remain hopeful that this can be achieved. More importantly, due to inequalities in representation, power imbalances and corporate influence, the 'inside' debates are constrained within a business as usual framework. Meetings behind closed doors, dismissal of proposals that are not market-oriented, manipulation of documents, powerful influences from corporate lobbies and mainstream NGOs, amongst others, are all key concerns with this now evidently undemocratic platform. So should social movements reject the UN? And if we dismiss the only official international negotiating space with the power (at least in theory) to regulate polluting industries, how can these practices be halted?

Achieving climate justice is widely understood to be impossible through institutional means. Fabricio Guamán, referring to the UN and COP processes, said; "The outcomes of these conferences and accords will always be in the interests of the companies who are behind them, that's why I am convinced that they cannot reach climate justice. Another reason why they will not bring climate justice is the problem of participation; it is difficult to participate in decisions made at this level, and governments in the South like Ecuador do not have the same power or influence as for example governments like the United States. More strongly put, I believe they work against climate justice."

Of those we spoke to in Cochabamba almost everyone responded definitively that the UN process will not be useful in bringing about climate justice. As Soumitra Ghosh stated, "Climate Justice is only possible through effective people's processes that do not depend upon inter-governmental and corporate shows". Years of failing climate negotiations have led people to lose hope in these processes, and many now see them as acting only to expand the capitalist system. Severino Sharupe told us these institutions and processes make it incapable of creating real solutions; "The UN is not trustable. The people inside the UN have the same worldviews that the movements are trying to challenge, this makes it impossible that it can be an institution that brings any change."

So how is the UN acting to reinforce this worldview? Colin Rajah points to the structures of inequality between the 'rich' and 'poor' countries embedded within these processes: "The richer countries are really controlling the process in such a way that any changes that are made are going to be incremental at best, and we've seen that happening in Copenhagen." However, this issue is of course intertwined with the issue of representation within countries; as Jimmy Cruz explains, "the proposals and solutions that are born from the population, from the same citizens, with great difficulty or on few occasions arrive at a table of the presidency. Very rarely are they heard, almost never." The historic and current imbalances of power between and within countries result in a situation where the dominant capitalist worldview is not only maintained and strengthened, but also the countries that are most threatened by the consequences of climate change and have less resources to confront it are being pushed into negotiations where their voices are not heard.

Other crucial problems identified with the UN process are the co-optation of the negotiations by transnational corporations, and mainstream NGOs claiming to speak on behalf of 'civil society' while legitimising and encouraging the false market solutions. Most corporations publicly present themselves as part of the solutions with 'business-friendly' proposals. Few continue to voice opposition to any action to combat climate change, but instead push for technologies and markets that will allow them to maintain and expand their polluting practices under a 'green' capitalism. Corporate lobbies are highly influential in governmental decisions. As Fabricio Guamán affirmed, "the outcomes of these conferences and accords will always be in the interest of the companies who are behind them."

Moreover, the influence of several international NGOs coalesced mostly under the 'tcktcktck' campaign, are reinforcing existing power relations and capitalist (non)solutions by legitimising market mechanisms that movements fiercely opposed during the Peoples' Summit. In some cases, NGOs like WWF and International Conservation have gone further by creating labels for 'good projects' under the carbon market schemes which support the greenwashing efforts of polluters. "The UN treats the big NGOs as representing 'civil societies' and social movements. Cochabamba shows that there is another way. Who gives these big NGOs the legitimacy to speak for the people they say they are representing?" (Leonardo Cerdo).

The false solutions being pushed by mainstream NGOs and corporations mean that the peoples suffering the consequences of this system are facing an even worse situation. Market mechanisms have exacerbated land-grabs and large-scale projects while allowing polluters to continue business-as-usual. "If you see the last ten years, what has come from these organizations is nothing in terms of improving people's lives, so I don't think these are the places where we should put our efforts. I think this shouldn't be the social movements' agenda... our work should be on a different level, on different strategies." (Marcela Olivera)

However, despite all these problems, some people point to the fact that the UN is an existing institution, and to ignore it is to ignore a powerful decision making space. As Alejandra Escobar understands it, "any space where decisions are made is a space of struggle. We as a movement should be present in all the different spaces; this means working inside as well as outside the system during the COP process". However, she added that real changes are difficult to make happen inside since the political lines are being defined by corporations. To some people though, movements can use these spaces tactically towards our own goals of climate justice. Fabricio Guamán believes that "social movements can reveal the contradictions of the discourse at this level; they can give a face to the companies who are behind these conferences, financing and supporting them, as well as exposing the NGOs these companies are financing to work in their interest."

So although crucial problems are identified with the UN process there is an apparent difference of opinion over whether there is anything to be gained from focusing energies on it. Some feel that there are ways of engaging with these spaces that can have direct results in preventing some of the worst damaging policies from being implemented and making antagonisms more visible. Others are of the view that the UN is fundamentally flawed and any efforts to influence it would be better used on entirely separate processes. Despite this difference there is undoubtedly a consensus that the systemic changes that are required cannot be brought about through these institutions.

"Climate justice can be brought about only by confronting and decomposing the powers that drive the process." (Sabu Kosho)

The failure of COP-15 last December has of course drawn greater focus on processes outside the UN, such as the CMPCC. Fabricio Guamán remarked that "these conferences can also be used strategically by the movement to create better and stronger networks, and to learn how to work together better and create unity among ourselves." And this is exactly what was happening at the CMPCC according to Christian Guerrero; "Cochabamba was an example of how social movements can act independently of the UN process. Cochabamba offers a lot of strong ideas, around the rights of mother earth for example. We need to see how they can be realised. We need to put things into action."

Notwithstanding the differences, there was a common call from those we spoke to for bottom up, autonomous solutions and for social movements to concentrate their efforts on effecting real change outside of official channels. It is beyond the remit of this booklet to consider what other forms of struggle could be effectively adopted to build these worlds outside of capitalism. However as we reject the UN process a desire for a transnational space for strategising seems to be emerging. Whether the CMPCC can provide this in the longer term very much depends on the answers to the following questions.

ix.

HISTORY OF COP

In 1972, the UN Conference on Human Environment in Stockholm marked the beginning of intergovernmental negotiations to address environmental problems, however, filled with economic interests it heavily promoted market development. Later on, the so-called 'Brundtland Commission' issued in 1987 the report 'Our Common Future' correlating the idea of sustainable development in line with economic growth. Following the same direction, the Earth Summit in 1992 in Rio, Brazil established the UN Framework Convention on Climate Change (UNFCCC), which entered into force in 1994 with the ratification of 165 countries. An accomplishment gained by the G77 and China block with the UNFCCC was its subscription to the 'common but differentiated responsibilities' principle, which recognises that although climate change is a common problem there are different responsibilities among countries due to the historical emissions that led to the accumulation of wealth by industrialised countries. However, the convention promoted the idea of 'sustainable development through trade liberalization' and gave a 'positive role' to corporations.

The US, steadily affirming that the international response had to be guided by efficiency and cost-effectiveness, proposed in 1995 at the first Conference of the Parties (COP) in Berlin, the use of market mechanisms that would help industrialised countries to reach their targets. Later on, in 1997 during the COP-3 in Kyoto, Japan, the Kyoto Protocol was created, setting binding targets for industrialised countries that could be reached by the use of 3 market mechanisms: Emissions Trading (ET), Joint Implementation (JI) and the Clean Development Mechanism (CDM). However, various issues of implementation and regulation were left open.

Under ET industrialised countries receive an initial allocation of tradable credits that can be bought and sold among them under the Protocol as a market commodity (known as 'cap-and-trade'). Therefore, if a corporation needs to emit above its permitted level, it can buy credits to cover this increase. It also allows trading with the credits acquired under the CDM and the JI.

The CDM emerged from a Brazilian proposal to create a 'Clean Development Fund' that would apply penalties for industrialised countries that exceeded their targets in order to finance climate mitigation and adaptation projects in the geographical South. However, during COP-3, the Fund was transformed into a market Mechanism and fines were transformed into prices. Currently, the CDM allows polluting governments and corporations to implement 'clean' (cheap) projects in the geographical South (large-scale plantations, windfarms, mega-dams, efficiency improvement in coal-fired plants, etc.) in order to buy credits that can 'offset' their emission reduction obligations or sold in the financial markets. As a result, while the climate criminals can pay their way out of any responsibility and make more money out of it, offset projects are causing severe social and environmental problems while dispossessing many communities from their territories and cultures. The JI applies the same idea of the CDM but the projects are localised mostly in Eastern Europe.

The Kyoto Protocol was ratified and entered into force in 2005. It 'binds' industrialised countries to reduce from 2008 to 2012 their emissions by an average of 5.2 per cent from 1990 levels. Yet, the core deal was held together with the creation of the CDM as the only mechanism that involves developing countries, which has been operational since 2006. Although the Kyoto Protocol was established under the UNFCCC, the 'common but differentiated responsibilities' principle has been turned around by imposing more burden on developing countries.

The world's largest 'cap and trade' scheme is the European Union Emissions Trading System (EU ETS), which began in 2005. It covers 30 countries, including the 27 EU member states, plus Norway, Iceland and Lichtenstein. In the first phase of the scheme (2005-2008) far too many emissions credits were handed out to industries mainly as a result of corporate lobbying, and thus, the 'cap' did not cap anything. The over-allocated credits plus the offset credits bought in the market collapsed the price of carbon credits, yet they generated huge 'windfall profits' for power producers. The same problems are happening in the second phase of the scheme, which runs from 2008-2012. Yet the EU's Emissions Trading Scheme exists independently of any COP decision.

The UN negotiations involve many more actors than governmental representatives. Corporate lobbies have a crucial role (and many interests) in the climate negotiations. They have been preventing any regulation that could become costly and therefore promote 'business-friendly' (non)solutions as well as strategic 'alliances' with mainstream NGOs, governments and the UN itself. At the same time, multilateral financial institutions are key players for setting up and boosting the carbon markets, even though many Indigenous and forest dependent communities have rejected the intervention of specifically the World Bank, (WB).

During the COP-13 in Bali, Indonesia, two-year negotiation tracks agreed to reach a post-2012 climate agreement by 2009, during COP-15. The key issues were: mitigation, adaptation, technology and finance. Massive protests filled the streets in Bali demanding that the environment was taken out of markets and the WB out of the forests. The network Climate Justice Now! was formed and declared, "Inside the negotiations, the rich industrialised countries have put unjustifiable pressure on Southern governments to commit to emissions reductions... Once again, the majority world is being forced to pay for the excesses of the minority."[15]

As it was evident, COP-15 in Copenhagen last December was far from reaching an agreement. The (non) accord was made by 26 political leaders. There were attempts to impose it, but there were rejected by Bolivia, Venezuela, Sudan, Nicaragua and Tuvalu'. Bolivia called out for a Peoples' Summit in April as a response to the failure of Copenhagen.[16] The next round of negotiations will be held in Cancun, Mexico (see box 16b).

The climate debate is playing an instrumental role in re-affirming a 'green new deal' that is pushing capitalism further with the expansion of markets and the further enclosure of nature. An hegemonic ideology based on 'green capitalism' is expanding the privatisation of the commons in the name of 'combating climate change', while strengthening the political and economic structures of the current unsustainable system. Once again, the geographic and political global south is already being affected not only by the consequences of climate change itself but also by the climate policies and mechanisms that are imposing a new colonialism on local territories and cultures.

<15> climate-justice-now.org/category/events/bali/

<16> http://pwccc.wordpress.com/2010/06/16/comparision-of-the-people%C2%B4s-agreement-and-the-copenhagen-accord/

7C. TO DANCE WITH THE DEVIL?
"What are the possibilities and dangers of social movements cooperating with governments' and the state?"

Called by a government that despite its radical rhetoric still has a police force, an army, prisons and does business with imperialists, the CMPCC was layered with complexities and contradictions. Although 'the state' and its relationship to society is not a new discussion among movements, the Latin American and in particular the Bolivian historical process has led movements to develop different relations with and rejections of the state. Some are more sceptical than others. We are not arguing that this or the other is the way for real transformation, but we consider it important to reflect on how these questions are fundamental for achieving transnational connections among movements.

Many of our interviewees drew on their own bitter experiences to argue that the dangers of working with the state far outweigh the potential benefits, especially in the long term. This echoes our own collective view. However, as described in the introduction, we did not go to Bolivia to reinforce previously held beliefs, but to listen and to use the moment of the summit to look at the interplay between the government and movements in Bolivia. This section attempts to contribute to an understanding of how movements are interacting with states within specific contexts and the risks that this involves for the process of transformation. Although this section does draw heavily on the CMPCC, we hope that it also has broader resonance. We will present and reflect upon a series of responses we received from the people we spoke to, considering first some of the possibilities and then some of the dangers that were highlighted.

"The CMPCC had great potential to bring together the critical edge of environmental and social movements" (Nick Buxton).

The summit in Cochabamba stood as an example of social movements and the state collectively articulating radical discourses to be inserted into international arenas such as the UNFCCC and the COP process. The space, organisation and infrastructure were provided by the government and the demands and the content, to a reasonable extent, came from below. There was greater space to meet and plan than at many counter-summit mobilisations, where direct confrontation with the state can sap time and energy. "There is a false consensus, probably from the media, that these solutions can only happen at the governmental or intergovernmental level. Cochabamba was an example of how social movements can act independently of the UN process and offer a lot of strong ideas, around the rights of mother earth for example," (Cristian Guerrero). With the space provided, people were able to develop key demands at the global level. The idea is that these movements "Can go back and use this framework, and then adapt it to their local struggles." (Nick Buxton)

In the MAS administration, contact between ministries and social movements occurs on a daily basis, and many feel that there is a real ability to influence national policy. As Evo says, "I learned in this short time being President, that it's best to govern subordinate to our peoples, that its best to govern understanding and meeting the demands of our peoples, and that the most important is a participatory democracy where our people decide." The CMPCC could possibly be seen as an attempt to internationalise and spread awareness of this approach and the radical discourse that can emerge as a result.

"In the times of neoliberal trans-nationals, our native authorities were denied to enter the vice ministries or the central government. Today, we have the priority as indigenous, as native authorities... Since our president, indigenous as we are, took control over the central government, we have been listened to" (Florian Quispe Flores).

There a difference between working with, and actually becoming part of the state. It is a common view in Bolivia that a long period of disenfranchisement ended with the entry of indigenous leaders into the government following the 2005 election. In the Latin American context of centuries of colonialism and the more recent imposition of neoliberal models of development, this recognition was talked about by many of the interviewees. "The government have tried to include the philosophy and religion, the indigenous vision, into their society, by including indigenous concepts like "Mother Earth" *(Pachamama)*, "Good Life" *(Buen Vivir)*, and nature and water rights" (Fabricio Guamán).

Carlos Crespo Flores, who has strong critiques of what is happening in Bolivia, explained that the arrival of Evo in the government, "has produced a change, at least, in the form of symbolic power. If you go to the *campesino* regions and compare it with what it was like before, five years ago, there is this collective self-esteem. And that's good, really good. But that's where we have got to and that's it, the symbolic dimension of the process." Can this symbolic power materialise into personal and collective empowerment? Or will it simply serve to calm, and soften, indigenous demands?

Of course processes and histories of de-colonisation are not unique to Bolivia, nor to Latin America. There are numerous examples of peoples moving towards national independence, seeking to undo the injustices and damages inflicted by colonialism and imperialism, and leaders elected to realise peoples' hopes for change. However, "The image of Evo Morales for any Latin American is very strong. It seems that is a revindication issue. It is as if we are saying 'We have to decolonise and here an Indigenous person is leading the way... The social and power relations are different than comparing it to countries like Mexico (where the government is right wing). When talking about Evo it is with much respect since he is (still) part of the grassroots communal bonds" (Mayeli Sanchez).

"In Bolivia, people have no fear to take down any government who are fucking shit up" (Alejandra Escobar).

Perhaps the most commonly referred to potential of social movements working with the state was the possibility of achieving actual changes in material conditions. Even when there is much more to achieve and aim for, we cannot underestimate the significance of improvements to social facilities, education, health, and sovereignty, and much of this can be in part attributed to pressure from below. Social movements have the potential to put states under strong pressure and overthrow governments. Bolivia's history of popular uprisings bringing down successive governments and throwing out multinational corporations is not easily forgotten. But how is it possible to move beyond states, to change the very foundations and social relations upon which they are based?

While movements have relied on ongoing self-organisation, autonomy and fights against repression, these factors can be adversely impacted by relationships with the state, even the apparently positive ones, and can cause divisions. A fragmented and fractured movement can more easily be co-opted or neutralised. The ongoing challenge for Bolivian social movements is how to retain their vitality and autonomy when pitted against a government that presents itself as aligned to their interests, i.e. anti-capitalist, anti-imperialist, of the people and indigenous.

The difference from previous administrations is that MAS is willing to open spaces for dialogue, even though is a difficult path. There is an acknowledgement that MAS has to respond the demands of the people, although clearly there are also numerous other interests, which are sometimes stronger. Evo has frequent meetings with the leaders of the 'Pacto de Unidad', a broad coalition formed in 2006 by strong movements, who make demands and push particular policies[17]. MAS ministers, congress people and Evo all visit, talk with and listen to communities. In this sense MAS is perceived as half-party, half-movement. The problem is that these spaces for dialogue are not autonomous from the government, and they are sometimes linked to the construction of public services, e.g. a school.

We experienced illustrative example of how even in one individual we see a blurring of what are often distinct political spheres in the Bolivian context. Three of us attended the CSTUCB *campesino* congress at the invitation of Cristian Domínguez, the secretary for natural resources and the environment for the confederation and part of the Bolivian platform on climate change that has been advising the government. Two of us had met him in the UK back in November 2009 as he was mobilising and calling for civil disobedience in Copenhagen.[18] As a delegate to the COP process from Bolivian social movements he was carrying out 'People's Diplomacy', travelling in Europe and putting forward the Bolivian position to social movements and civil society groups. As someone who is very much working inside these institutions but recognises the importance of linking up with those of us on the outside, he had come to action planning meetings in Copenhagen and helped to lead the walk out of the UN process trying to reach the Reclaim Power action. Not only this but he is now involved with the massive mobilisation to demand that the government defend the Amazon territory from being plundered by oil, logging and mining companies.[19]

The relations between state institutions and movements in Bolivia are dynamic, confusing and involve ongoing tensions and conflicts.

"*A radical position would be not to interact with (state) institutions. However, this is a way to isolate ourselves and lose contact with the people. That is why we have to struggle within the system as well*" (Alejandra Escobar).

This statement reflects the way that although grassroots movements are generally much closer to peoples' daily lives than governments, some Bolivians see the state as including 'the people' in some way. There are often practical reasons for having inside/outside strategies, if only to have access to powerful institutions, such as the school system. Some see it as important, "to be able to understand government systems and personalities in order to be...effectively creating change within that system" (Colin Rajah).

This sentiment reflects the fact that many are critical of the institutions of government, but in order to achieve concrete aims in the present they see pressuring them as a necessary evil; "Governments and states should be working for us, they are an extension of the communities they're in and we should be holding them accountable and calling them to task on that" (Colin Rajah). One example

[17] http://www.constituyentesoberana.org/info/?q=node/83local leaders,

[18] See story and video http://bristol.indymedia.org/article/691449

[19] Amazon Indigenous Communities Plan 1,000-km March http://www.ipsnews.net/news.asp?idnews=51462

given was of Sanctuary Cities in the US where, partly as a result of pressure from social movements, ordinance laws have been passed in over 30 major cities that police forces should not comply with federal laws that require them to question people about their immigration status. Another example given was Ecuador's 2008 constitution, being "like the skeleton of the different relationships of individuals and collectives in the state" (Fabricio Guamán), and the first in the world to recognise legally enforceable Rights of Nature. But despite this the government continues to pursue expansion of extractive industries at the expense of the environment and local communities.

> Whilst these reforms do not solve the root causes or resolve contradictions, they can provide some necessary relief. The question is if these partial successes can help or create spaces for fighting the root causes of the current crises.

"When social movements are represented within the state there is the possibility to diplomatically counteract, mitigate and, in certain circumstances, even prevent the abuse of power, corruption and the misuse of the coercive apparatus of the State machinery against progressive forces" (Sankofahamu Sankofa).

A decrease in the prevalence of state repression is one tangible advantage that should not be underestimated. But while physically violent repression of dissident voices may appear to have declined in Bolivia, repression remains, sometimes in more subtle forms. Once a state has been seen to be legitimised by the engagement of social movements, their statements against those who still offer up dissent are ever more dangerous.

"There is a real danger in trying to work closely with governments and states because we can get caught up in that system and caught up in the trappings of that" (Colin Rajah).

It emerged from several of the interviews that it was a very difficult balance to work to influence a state without being drawn into compromises. Colin Rajah used the case of NGOs to illustrate this, "NGOs who are well resourced end up compromising so much in order to gain their immediate organisational goals. That actually compromises what we're trying to do and what we're trying to achieve in the movement. So I think that level of cooperation and working together is ultimately very detrimental to what we're trying to accomplish".

At the same time some presented concerns about absolute positions that deny the possibility of a strategic and conscious interaction to serve a particular end. "Bolivian movements have navigated it pretty well, maintained their critique but engaged. And I think this is part of a model to learn from this example. I think at the same time we can be quite purist, social movements equals good, governments equals bad. Whilst of course within the social movements there are hierarchies and we need to democratise. We need to keep our critical faculties intact. It's not one option or the other" (Nick Buxton).

BEYOND MAKING DEMANDS – THE RIGHT TO WATER

In Bolivia the struggle over access to water is symbolic of the broader political context. Carlos Crespo Flores expands on some of the complexities of enacting a demand from the social movements.

> "One of the conditions that the social movements put to Evo to support his candidature was that he would create a Ministry of Water if he won….I formed part of the group that structured this Ministry so I have seen this process close up. Quickly I saw that they were replicating more of the same, taking the demands of the people and expropriating them. I left straight away and we started to take a critical attitude when we saw the effects around the theme of irrigation. We started to question this law publicly, saying – this has to change, because it is deepening inequalities in the world of the indigenous *campesinos*. It's creating a newly privileged class with water. And what was the attitude of the government and in particular the social leaders? The *regantes*[20], in one of their congresses in 2006 called us, the four professionals, enemies of the sector. They said we were allies of the right and they threw us out. This is the behaviour that we see. If you have a critical attitude about the process and reveal that, you are totally excluded, discredited, it's common that they do that.

The grassroots, yes they want change, that's why they supported Evo and why they still support him. They want something else, they are tired of politicians and the style of politics in Bolivia. But it's the leadership who is in there within corrupt relations. So… while they don't change these undemocratic structures, these practices, they aren't going to change anything… what we have is, these leaders again expropriating the desires of the people to serve other interests, which is what is happening now. It's frustrating what is happening, and truthfully I'm pessimistic that this is an interesting journey, don't fool yourself of that."

‹20› Regantes are those that work in irrigation and are one of the bases of support for the Evo government. From the Spanish verb, regar = to water.

'The Water is the People's' – graffiti Cochabamba

Any discussion of working with the state, leads us to ask where the power really lies. Whilst there are moments of potential through elected leaders to improve conditions, one of the fundamental roles of the state is to protect private property.

"States represent concrete capitalist interests; the state depends on capital as it needs the resources and jobs capital provides" (Fabricio Guaman).

We see the contradictions of capitalism playing out, "It is the Janus-headed nature of the state that I observed in Bolivia: the direct support of the government (MAS) to certain cooperative productions, while the drive for prosperity of the state causes environmental problems and immiseration of the people," (Sabu Kosho). Several of the people in the Bolivian ministry of economics are alumni of western economic schools and although they are making some reforms they are thoroughly steeped in the dominant economic logic. The key question, that we will consider further in the next section, is whether any government is able to change the overarching power structures or social relationships that underpin global capitalism.

When any movements consider working with the state, they must recognise the other powerful influences and allies that the state works with and represents. "What I see is that the dominant institutions in this world right now are not the governments or the state, but the corporations. And what I see is that these corporations have a lot of influence in the governments and the state so we should be very cautious about engaging in any process that has to sit with them, even if we're talking about progressive governments or states. For example Ecuador seems to be a very progressive state, but if you look into the reality there they have a lot of problems, the same as Bolivia" (Marcela Olivera). One example of this is how in a newspaper we read during the conference we saw how Linera, the vice president, was in New York trying to attract new investment and reassuring companies that their assets would be safe.

"The social movements follow the recipes that are coming from the state with no question at all" (Carlos Crespo Flores).

The powerful history of social movements in Latin America is an inspiration to many, who celebrate their radical positions and ability to propose real alternatives. However, many in Bolivia are seeing that long-term engagement with an ultimately authoritarian and controlling state is stifling the autonomy of social movements and eliminating their capacity to make proposals. The social movements brought Evo to power, but some see that this is leaving them weaker and less able to continue pushing for social change. Faced with calls for unity against both the threat of the right and the imperialist overlords the room for manoeuvre or articulation of radical proposals has diminished.

Whether this is because they actively support the broader political governmental project, are fearful of the alternative (in Bolivia's case a return to neoliberal/right wing state politics), or because they receive financial support, once social movements are working in (or with) the government it becomes less likely that they will deeply criticise. In this case, the social movements can "serve, consciously or unconsciously, as the auxiliary forces for the counter-revolutionary elements in the intelligence, security and other coercive organs of the repressive state machinery of questionably 'progressive' regimes. This is particularly true of those operating in the colonially designed and neo-colonially refurbished state machinery...in Afrika today"

(Sankofahamu Sankofa). State power and control has been developed over centuries and it is almost impossible to dismantle within the time frame of electoral politics, however Morales has not, so far, said that he is following that long-term aim.

While seen by some as a short-term mechanism of transition, the state can equally be furthering its own empowerment rather than effectively challenging or removing it. "What we propose is the rupture of this political structure, that house. What is happening is that here in Bolivia what they are doing is strengthening that house that was going downwards. We do not want to give strength to that house; we want to break down that house In order to construct a new house. That means to strengthen society, strengthen organised systems and strengthen collectivity, and from that, we can build" (Severino Sharupe).This reflects the understanding that lies at the base of anarchist/anti-authoritarian rejection of any kind of working with the state. Perhaps it is possible to develop a kind of parallel process where new governments can be formed without completely co-opting the social movements that helped put them there, but to our knowledge history contains no examples of this.

Some of the Bolivian social movements are not responsively democratic and have entrenched positions of leaders in power – Evo Morales being the best example of this. In 1985, Morales was elected general secretary in a union of coca farmers and by 1988 was elected executive secretary of the Tropics Federation, a position he retains to this day.

"If the structures do not change then it is the State who exploits... That means nothing has changed. Before they would do it, now we do it" (Fabricio Guaman).

This is permitted by the "Leftist, dogmatic vision, of our politicians, the ministers, the technicians, the organic intellectuals, to use the Gramscian term. They all come from this tradition, leftist, dogmatic, and nothing changes. They come from this experience, they carry on thinking the same, with an authoritarian vision of processes" (Carlos Crespo Flores). This calls into question any homogeneous view of social movements and the possibilities for changes that they can achieve. A social movement with internal hierarchies may fit more neatly into governmental relations and therefore be effective in achieving reforms. Autonomous and horizontal movements and networks try to be less easily manipulated or directed, but face a different set of challenges and informal hierarchies. It seems that vigilance is always required to guard against unaccountable spokespeople or entrenched leaders.

The examples of this happening and its devastating effects leave Sankofahamu Sankofa to warn that a danger of working with the state is that movements will begin "pimping off activists and encouraging their prostitution as hypocritical mouthpieces of mere governmental propaganda; susceptibility to anti-People corruption, bureaucratic careerism and elitism; degeneration into conduits of bourgeois capitalist reformism". Here we see the very complex interweaving of paths towards systemic transformations, which may 'dance with the devils' of governments and risk allowing a government to "speak for the movement" (Alejandra Escobar).

"What we want is a system change. Even if there is a government that could have good will or be progressive, it won't represent us" (Mayeli Sanchez).

The principle dangers of social movements working with the state can be seen to include those of being co-opted, enabling underlying power structures to remain intact, losing the power to oppose or facing repression if we do, and legitimising the very 'right to govern' that governments are predicated on. It is this inability, or even unwillingness, to make deep and lasting structural changes beyond mere rhetoric that explains the ultimate scepticism. Whilst "states could be a transition ultimately we say that in some moment the States will have to disappear. For some, states can seem as a strength but for others it can be a problem and also the current political structural causes for division" (Severino Sharupe).

In conversations in Bolivia, we were repeatedly told that this process of change is not about one man or one party but is about a broader project for change. We do not pretend here that those taking the decision to work in or with the government are unaware of the potential dangers. In a set of complex conditions of massive poverty and suffering and to achieve urgently needed reforms a government moving towards socialism is in a lot of ways an understandable and in the short-term an effective strategy. However, "the state cannot offer the final solution to any problem: It is the problem. The subject is the multitude of social movements and their relationships. As long as extra-governmental forces are capable of keeping their autonomy while working with governments and can continue to pressure them, it would be worth having their help. But the question is how long it can last" (Sabu Kosho).

If we allow ourselves to be fully subsumed in the rhetoric of 'urgency' and 'ultimate threat' to the world that abounds in climate related politics, there is risk of walking away from considered and strategic thought and action, and potentially into dangerous compromises. The current threats need to be urgently countered and solved whilst being understood as yet another impact of colonialism, capitalism and the politics of domination that have existed for centuries and have always needed dismantling. It is an important challenge that movements, if engaging with the state, hold it accountable on its 'promises'. Certainly just a few weeks after the CMPCC indigenous peoples of the Amazon region declared themselves in a 'state of emergency' and announced that they will march 1000-km to La Paz to demand that the government respect the constitution and defend their territory from being plundered by oil, logging and mining companies. "President Morales should listen and be sensitive to what is happening and rethink the course of change together with social movements" said indigenous leader Cristian Domínguez.

Recognising all the dangers and risks on this level of interaction, is it possible for the Bolivian government to maintain its rhetoric on 'Rights of Pachamama' without achieving any material change? It would certainly be hard to maintain legitimacy as the 'leader' of mother earth rights as these contradictions are exposed. Only time will tell, but things are constantly in flux. A new left wing party, *Movimiento Sin Miedo*, or Movement without Fear, is gaining support in previous MAS strongholds and there are increasing accusations that some in the government are becoming drunk with power and following the footsteps of the right. It could well be that the Bolivian social movements, once again, will be rethinking their relationships to the state.

"I truly feel, sisters and brothers, that capitalism is destroying the environment, and I am not mistaken and I don't have any fear in saying to the whole world, that the number one enemy of humans and of nature is capitalism, and the West must react to these systems and economic models that are destroying the environment" (Evo Morales Ayma).

7D. CAPITALISM OR LIFE?
"Is climate justice possible without moving beyond capitalist relations?"

In the light of Evo Morales' outspoken criticism of capitalism despite continued policies of industrial expansion, we were particularly curious to discuss this question with people on the front line of climate and anti-capitalist struggles. These conversations proved especially important in light of our understanding of climate justice, and brought out a number of themes to explore here.

Just as it became important to recognise that there exist different forms and understandings of capitalism, so too there are different forms anti-capitalism and different ideas as to how a future based outside of capitalist relations might look. Some of the people we spoke to were very clear that capitalism itself is not the only location of struggle. The relationship between humans and nature was considered by some to be fundamental to understanding and tackling capitalism and the climate crises.

The responses we received showed a basic common agreement that capitalism is one of the root causes of climate change, "These kinds of relationships that we have right now are all based on capital and money and transactions and that kind of exchange, so that's why we're having the problems right now with climate, with water and basically with everything that's causing conflict on the planet" (Marcela Olivera).

While there may have been agreement on capitalism as a root cause, the question of how to dismantle these relations remained an area of contestation. "How can we move away from the capitalist system? How we can shift away from these kind of neo-colonial imperialistic relationships that exist internationally right now?" (Colin Rajah).

Whilst countries such as Bolivia position themselves as clearly opposed to the global capitalist and neoliberal programme of the most polluting countries, they continue to be tied into relationships of extraction and trade in order to fund their programme of socialist redistribution. "It's not just capitalism. Tendencies of industrialisation, modernisation and consumerism can happen without capitalism. Venezuela and Bolivia are good examples of this – it is over romanticised to say it is just anti-capitalism – Bolivia and Venezuela have a big role to play in this as they are sitting on huge reserves of fossil fuels" (Christian Guerrero).

There appears then, for some, a tangible difference between having anti-capitalist rhetoric or ideals and actually being able to exist wholly outside of capitalist relations. Similarly we can't help but recognise the contradictions between what we believe in and our own daily realities. "Our presidents have a very strong anti-imperial rhetoric, but at the same time they do very good business with the imperialists" (Carlos Crespo Flores).

The Bolivian context requires us to understand the different realities and conditions under which states and societies are operating. Unlike states of the geographical north, 'progressive' governments of the south have a lot of work to do in trying to redress the historical economic and geopolitical imbalances that have been produced under colonial and imperial powers for the benefit of capitalism. Further, the process of change in Bolivia does not happen within a vacuum, and remains under constant threat from both internal right-wing forces and the international hegemonic forces that resource and support these challenges.

For many, the fight against capitalism and the private property rights that underpin it is more than just a question of economics. Fabricio Guáman, who has fought on the front lines of territory and climate struggles, told us that oil extraction for him is demonstrative of a completely antagonistic way of seeing the world. "The capitalist world lets us think that we can negotiate, but we cannot- not because we are radicals and don't want to, but because we don't speak the same language... the concept of 'Good Living' *(Buen Vivir)* does not coexist with oil extraction... And so you will lose the battle when you start negotiating with them, the government or the oil companies, because then you accept the possibility that they destruct the 'Good Living.'"

This is indicative of how capitalist relations are not solely economic relations, it becomes more clear how globalised capitalism has used as a strategy the on-going physical and psychological separation of human beings from the natural environment. In this way they have created cultures and practices in which the natural environment and natural resources are only considered of 'value' when they are commodified: extracted, priced and sold in markets. "I don't think this is present so much in climate justice movements in the north: seeing climate change as a symptom of the breakdown of the relationship between humans and nature" (Nick Buxton).

This can be seen as one of the key drivers behind indigenous peoples' continued struggles to reject relations based on material accumulation – a position that is often on the margins of the dominant cultures in which they live. "Indigenous people have a different cosmovision and other ways of living which are not comprehensible with capitalism. The people of the Amazon have other ways to relate to one another which are not focused on profit and money." (Fabricio Guamán)

In this regard, Severino Sharupe told us how these same capitalist relations are permeating indigenous lives and changing their cultural approach, "There is a very strong wave that is transforming people towards a destructive way of living... this capitalist system is changing the structures of thought. It makes us think that the solution is to have big enterprise, to loot what is underground, that through money our problems can be solved, and not to realise what the fundamental elements of life are. I am astonished by how much everything is about buy and sell, everything turns to money. Why there cannot exist other ways?"

However, as Marcela Olivera warned us, it is also important not to romanticise different cultures, nor view their cultures as static, "It's not about recovering what the indigenous people believe. It's more about what's happening right now and how we can create solutions based on the actual reality, not on stereotypes."

Graffiti Cochabamba

In Bolivia, the tensions between traditional ancestral practices and the realities of modern day financial conditions are clearly evident. Much of the state's socialist programmes are paid directly from the profits earned by the same carbon-intensive and environmentally destructive practices that fuel the global capitalist infrastructure and are responsible for causing climate change, albeit occurring under (partially) nationalised companies. "In Bolivia, they talk about the need for industrialisation, but we shouldn't enter into the web of global capital" (Alejandra Escobar). Many participants could not ignore the contradictions of the Bolivian state calling for the rights of mother earth (or Pachamama) whilst maintaining polluting practices so destructive of the environment such as mining, mega-dams or REDD-type projects (see chapter 5). While it is clear that the most polluting states require the biggest changes, it is worrying to see that the Great Industrial Leap is being pursued by Bolivia.

This tension calls us to consider- how do we imagine a future world free from capitalist relations and environmentally destructive practices, and what steps might we take to get there? The current position of the Bolivian state could be seen by some as a short-term engagement with extractive industries on the road to a total transformation of national economic and political relations, whilst others warn that this is merely a movement towards a new form of extractivism and domination, albeit with a different distribution of resources along the way.

Some people were determined of the necessity of a combined approach: "How can we strategically use the system whilst undermining it at the same time? It's a really critical time, we can't just say that what we need is a more radical proposal, but we also need to think about what we can deliver now as well.

Whilst it is best to root our struggles locally, we will need some state initiatives. We need to be strategic and keeping in mind the power relations" (Nick Buxton). However, others were less forgiving: "For states and governments there are no alternatives to this model, the only thing of importance is the extraction in the capitalist system." (Fabricio Guamán)

The discussions around this topic triggered some important questions: Is the fight against capitalism as the root cause of climate change the same as the fight to stop the extraction of fossil fuels? Leaving fossil fuels in the ground could surely mean the end of global capitalism as we know it, and would certainly cause the collapse of our current industrial production practices and the abundance of cheap energy they demand. But while the market continues to look for ways of profiting from this crisis, agrofuels, nuclear power, hydroelectric large-scale dams, REDD projects and many more so called 'alternatives' to fossil fuels are equally environmentally and socially destructive, being based on the same processes of commodification, privatisation, appropriation and exploitation of natural resources, with the violence and domination necessary to facilitate them that capitalism necessitates.

It is clear that re-localising energy and food production are a major area of struggle to address climate injustice. But this alone will not stop exploration and extraction of fossil fuels for profit. Despite Evo's apparent conviction that capitalism is the number one enemy, his continuation of this extractive model of development questions the ability of any state to operate outside of this system.

7E. THE MEANING OF SOLIDARITY

"What does solidarity mean, and how can we work together more effectively to build the transnational struggle for climate justice? What are your views on the 'global south' and 'global north' and their relationships to struggle?"

"Unlike solidarity, which is horizontal and takes place between equals, charity is top-down, humiliating those who receive it and never challenging the implicit power relations."[21]

As people involved in social movements, we must constantly ask ourselves what it means to act and to be in solidarity, and with whom we form our alliances. Crucially, we must reflect on what we mean by the terms 'global south / global north,' because they are used a lot in many of the discussions of climate justice: What is their historical significance? Are they a useful political concept for movements? What does it mean to use these terms, and perhaps most importantly, what are the dangers of using these terms?

It is clear that one way to respond to the multiple crises we face is through working together in a way that looks to turn our diversity into a productive force for change rather than an obstacle. The responses that we received to this question point to the importance of rejecting simple geographical divisions and to understand the mutual learning and understanding that is required to act in solidarity with diverse movements against capitalism.

<21> Galeano, E. 2000 Upside Down: A Primer for the Looking Glass World. Picador, p. 312

First we will consider the meaning of the terms North and South. The global south is usually used to refer to all those states, predominantly located in the southern hemisphere, that have had a history of colonial exploitation and wealth transfer to states in the global north. There is undoubtedly a historical tendency towards the net transfer of economic wealth, on a global scale, from peoples and lands in the geographic south to a global elite, predominantly based in the geographic north. The entirety of Latin America, Africa, and large parts of Asia have had both their peoples and natural resources exploited by a handful of predominantly European empires and US interventions.

Whilst the complexities of race and class are beyond our remit here, it is significant that whilst colonialist expansion was initially driven by the mercantile search for resources, the racialised understanding of a hierarchy based on skin colour was central to defending its continuation and its worst brutalities. Today, this exploitation continues mostly under the auspices of transnational companies which, despite lacking an allegiance to specific states, continue to facilitate a net transfer of wealth towards an elite based predominantly in the geographical north.

This history of exploitation has led to very real differences in the 'actually existing' conditions of those in the north and south. The net transfer of wealth has apparently divided the globe along geographic lines – there exists real divisions in economic wealth between countries in the geographic south (such as most of South America, Africa and Asia) and the geographic north (aka the 'West'). However, this dynamic cannot be reduced down to an issue of geography. In the words of Sankofahamu Sankofa, "the terms 'global south' and 'global north' have meaning to us only as constructs for understanding and duly taking into account the concrete particularities, specifics and diverse realities of our common transnational Struggle for Global Justice... as shaped by the concrete dynamics of the history."

The concrete division in the realities of the global south/north are in fact a result of the appropriation of the global commons. In other words, states of the north are responsible for the political facilitation of capitalist expansion, whether that be through crude empires such as the Iberians in Latin America, or whether it be through forcing neoliberal policies through institutions such as the World Bank, IMF and WTO. However, the expansion of the social relations of capital with a globally exploited class is not however something divided uniquely along geographic lines. As Alejandra Escobar notes, "the countries of the North are relatively rich compared to the countries in the South. However, now we have countries rising in economic power as well. There are people in processes of struggle in all parts of the world."

This raises serious questions about the use of geographical divisions in conceptualising our forms of resistance, as maintaining the simplistic "view of global north/global south can really skew what we are trying to work for as we are trying to work as transnational movements and networks" (Christian Guerrero). Despite differing political perspectives, many of those we spoke to went beyond this crude geographical division through referring to the 'north in the south, and the south in the north', understanding that north/south is "not just a geographical" division of peoples and lands but "a really political construction" that places people into distinct categories of 'us' and 'them' (Colin Rajah). This concretely reminds of the massive inequality within the wealthiest nations, the growing so called, 'underclass' of people who live in extreme poverty, the people without papers, the criminalised and those who are unable for whatever reason to sell their labour.

Rather than being geographically based, the (re)creation of the global exploited, and the separation between the 'haves' and 'have nots', is something that occurs across the globe. In other words, the expropriation of the common is not limited to the expropriation of the geographical south to the benefit of the geographical north. Whilst there is a clear tendency due to historical processes towards this geographical flow of wealth, expropriation and accumulation is not a geographical process but one of exploiting what is shared by all for the benefit of the few. "Like the Achuar leader from Ecuador says: the struggles in the North and in the South against mega-projects are the same struggle against capitalism" (Laura López).

Given that our struggle is one of life against capital and its effects, how are we to truly act in solidarity? How do we ensure that we pay attention to the very real differences people experience across the globe, and do not fall into crude reductionism? An awareness of this danger means the first step in doing solidarity is to "understand how we can relate to each other. There have been experiences where the link has not strengthened movements and sometimes, these links insert movements into agendas that were not theirs and into dynamics that lead them to rupture" (Mayeli Sánchez Martinez).

Capital and the enclosure of the common is our enemy in all parts of the world, but it manifests itself in strikingly different ways. It is not enough to proclaim oneself 'anti-capitalist', we must "work together as movement for justice at every level. Maybe the word is not solidarity, its about mutual understanding" (Leonardo Cerda). This means we must listen and understand the struggles people are facing, whether it be against Monsanto lobbying for seed patents and reducing biodiversity, the physical repression of ones sexuality, or the struggle for education or healthcare. It is crucial that we recognise the specifics of each of these struggles, and consequently, the many solutions required that cannot be prescribed from elsewhere. We may face a single enemy in capital, but while our struggles are shared, they are not homogeneous.

"When speaking about struggle of social movements: it doesn´t matter where you are, North or South: everybody should construct a dignified life, create the possibility to decide for themselves, to choose the life you want. First you have to change and create your own structures and only then you should look to the rest of the world" (Fabricio Guáman).

Those in the geographical north can sometimes be blind to the fact that many "people in the south think that life in the north is paradise, though this is far from the truth" (Fabricio Guáman). Important struggles happen all around the world, and we must "take a step out on a limb and speak the truth about the underbelly of first world industrial civilisation" (Jack Herranen). In doing so, and in communicating the reality of northern-based struggles with those elsewhere, we break the myth that the 'developed' nations are a land of plenty to be desired.

The collective realisation must however go both ways. Those in the north must also be aware of the "tendency to idealise some of the things happening in countries such as Bolivia and Ecuador," as such an idealisation "doesn't help people who are trying to ramp up a constructive critique" (Jack Herranen). To take the recent experience of Bolivia, it is crucial that we listen to critical voices, such as those emerging from the Mesa 18, who reveal the tensions and problems that people are facing. The solidarity we are looking to create is not at all between nation-states, but among people struggling around the world.

A demo in Cochabamba to demand that water is installed in the outlying areas

"In the Amazon, solidarity is more than a word; it is a feeling and a way of living. It is to know that you are not alone, that you are not irresponsible. It is not only about other people but about everything. The words solidarity and reciprocity also mean respecting and taking care of the environment. In our way of life there exists a strong interdependence that functions against individualism. The capitalist system, that does not work, wants us to be isolated and only think in individuals. Solidarity can break the structure of this system if we all work together, collaborate and unite. The answer therefore is in the idea of cooperation" (Fabricio Guáman).

It is important for us to continue and deepen our conversations, and to collectively explore the ways in which this 'reciprocal solidarity' can manifest itself. Most importantly, "if we want to work together as a global movement we need to have a mutual understanding, not based on guilt. We need to view each other as equals without forgetting how we got to this situation" (Leonardo Cerda). This means moving beyond the internalisation of guilt amongst those living in the global north towards those living in the global south; we must understand our historical specificities, but we must also understand all that holds us together.

As one of the participants in our workshop 'Freedom of Movement in an age of climate chaos' said, "The borders that divide us exist primarily in the collective imagination but their impact ruptures our ability to imagine ourselves as a collective." It is this work of breaking down the socialisations of ourselves within these categories that makes the work of transnational solidarity so challenging and yet so ultimately important.

The opening ceremony of the CMPCC

8.

ANALYSIS OF AN EVENT

Taking all these responses into consideration and reflecting the conversations that we have had about the CMPCC we will now attempt to explain some of the outcomes and what this may mean for the future.

It is clear that one of the intentions of those that convened the CMPCC conference was to expose the UN climate summits as unrepresentative and undemocratic whilst also shaking up the COP process and exposing the dangers of the Copenhagen (non)accord. This was a continuation of Bolivia's strategy at previous COP meetings. Whilst we have criticisms of the conference, we recognise its value and the importance of the contents of the People's Accord, particularly when compared to UNFCCC discussions. It rejects carbon trading, offsets and GM as false solutions, draws attention to forced migration and calls for reversal of repressive immigration policies, whilst at the same time articulating calls for food and water sovereignty. This has created space for ongoing work around these issues but it is too early to judge what the longer term impacts will be. Given that it comes from an entirely different world view, it is not surprising that it was ignored during the UN meeting in Bonn. But when seen as part of a long term strategy to refocus and re-politicise the debate there has been some progress. Here we will reflect on the impacts of the conference and the shortfalls.

The most visible outcome and indeed the stated aim of the conference was the 'Peoples' Agreement'1, an eleven page document that synthesised the outputs of all seventeen working groups. A statement on the CMPCC website explains that "The "People´s Agreement" stems from an integral vision of climate change, incorporating the issue of the structural causes of the climate crisis, the rupture of harmony with nature,

THE PEOPLES' AGREEMENT

the need to recognise the rights of Mother Earth in order to guarantee human rights, the importance of creating a Tribunal of Climate and Environmental Justice, the development of global democracy so that the people can decide on this issue affecting the planet and all of humanity.'[22]. It is a unique document, both in terms of how it was produced and in terms of its content.

However, it is important to ask who are 'the people' that are making this declaration, who is it for, and why was it created? From the outset, it was stated that this conference, amongst other aims, was designed 'to agree on proposals for new commitments to the Kyoto Protocol and projects for a COP Decision under the United Nations Framework for Climate Change'. This is reflected in the Peoples' Agreement, which includes statements about desired caps for temperature rises. For example it calls for a limit of 1 degree rise in global average temperatures, and

[22] pwccc.wordpress.com/support

returning levels of greenhouse gases to 300ppm (parts per million). This is an extremely tough target, perhaps even unachievable given the temperature rises that have already occurred, and further warming we are committed to due to CO2 already in the atmosphere.[23] The justification for the target, given in the Shared Vision working group, is that given the severity of impacts at current levels of warming any further increases would be unacceptable and would risk 'irreversible changes' and declining global food production.

The inclusion of these targets shows that the document is looking to impact formal COP negotiations towards more stringent temperature limits. In this light, 'the people' is a legitimising tool to put weight behind positions that get little to no airtime within the formal negotiating processes. This is not necessarily a negative thing, but it suggests that a further interrogation of why 'the people' were mobilised is necessary. The language of formal and technical negotiations is of course meaningless to the majority of the world's 'people', where the actually existing crises of melting glaciers, reduced food yields and rising sea levels pose a concrete and very real threat.

On the other hand, this document contains many radical perspectives which are completely unrealisable with the current framework of official negotiations. It is quite unlikely that UN will adopt and take as its remit the statement that 'humanity confronts a great dilemma: to continue on the path of capitalism, depredation, and death, or to choose the path of harmony with nature and respect for life'. Whilst it would be interesting to see how the UN would operate according to this remit, it is probably safe for us to assume that we need not over-theorise this particular scenario. Of course, it is probable that those drafting the document were well aware of the limitations of influencing the UNFCCC and have cast desirable, even reasonable, yet impossible demands in attempt to discredit the entire COP process.

Finally, it is important to not erase the role of the state in this document. Whilst most of the content was made directly as the result of popular participation – most notably the rejection of REDD – there remain references to state led initiatives, despite opposition from participants. Part of the People's Accord refers to building a 'Global People's Movement for Mother Earth':

'In order to coordinate our international action and implement the results of this "Accord of the Peoples," we call for the building of a Global People's Movement for Mother Earth, which should be based on the principles of complementarity and respect for the diversity of origin and visions among its members, constituting a broad and democratic space for coordination and joint worldwide actions'...'Finally, we agree to undertake a Second World People's Conference on Climate Change and the Rights of Mother Earth in 2011 as part of this process of building the Global People's Movement for Mother Earth and reacting to the outcomes of the Climate Change Conference to be held at the end of this year in Cancún, Mexico.'

A further statement to the UN entitled 'Pronouncement of the World Peoples' Movement' suggests that the Bolivian government has chosen to pursue the goal of some kind of formalised 'peoples' movement', which it conceptualises as being based on 'principles of complementarity and respect for diversity.' Nonetheless, such a proposal is a cause for concern amongst many movements, especially those who experienced the Zapatista inspired 'horizontalism' of the past fifteen years. The proposal to form an institution to coordinate social movements, presented in the

[23] Wigley TML (2005) 'The climate change commitment'. Science 307:1766–1769; Meehl GA, et al. (2005) 'How much more global warming and sea level rise?' Science 307:1769–1772.

initial draft of the strategy document, was strongly rejected by La Via Campesina, the Landless Movements and others who said that if such a body was to form, it could not be instigated by a government and must come from below; a 'World Peoples' Movement' cannot be a state led initiative.

There were several other results from the CMPCC including calls for a declaration of the rights of mother earth, a world referendum on climate change and a tribunal for crimes against mother earth, but it is difficult to judge how successful these projects will be. For example, within the Latin American context a referendum makes sense, as it is a part of the political tradition of the region. Yet in other parts of the world, such as Europe, given current public discourse on climate change it is difficult to see how it would be of value. In many cases it may be a matter of supporting some of the principles behind the declaration and those expressed in the CMPCC, and translating them to appropriate language for different cultural contexts. This could involve re-thinking relationships with the natural environment, exploring the concept of 'the common', and finding ways of interweaving ecological thinking with existing social struggles.

Ultimately, what has been produced is a document that mixes specialist knowledge, movements' desires for another world, and state mediation. To reduce the process and the document down to anything less than this is misrepresentation of a participatory process that raised more questions than it answered. Furthermore, this document speaks to a broad audiences, to the UNFCCC in the first instance, but also to movements. The question is whether movements – people – choose to use it, and what the implications of this would be.

IMPACT AT THE UN

Within a week of the final Peoples' Agreement having been completed, a formal version was submitted to the UNFCCC by member nations of ALBA and representatives of social movements. The Official Submission made only superficial changes to the Peoples' Agreement, effectively making it a 'slim-downed' version. It was clearly intended to act as a counterbalance to the Copenhagen (non)accord, stating that if it became an agreement it could lead to as much as a 4 degree centigrade increase in global average temperatures this century. On top of this, mitigation under the (non)accord would fundamentally rely on carbon-markets, voluntary and individual commitments, and a central role for REDD – all of which were denounced in the Peoples' Agreement. It also provides an alternative vision for what an international deal should look like, positing solutions such as open technology transfer, adequate adaptation funds and the creation of an international climate tribunal.

As explained earlier, even though the Copenhagen (non)accord was only 'taken note of' by the UN, it has been used to try to manipulate countries into accepting various conditions on access to resources and to break up negotiating blocs such as the G77. The Peoples' Agreement also attempts to counter the divisive and coercive nature of the (non)accord:

'The "Copenhagen Accord" imposed on developing countries by a few States, beyond simply offering insufficient resources, attempts as well to divide and create confrontation between peoples and to extort developing countries by placing conditions on access to adaptation and mitigation resources. We also assert as unacceptable the attempt in processes of international negotiation to classify developing countries for their vulnerability to climate change, generating disputes, inequalities and segregation among them'.

Whilst the COP16, to be held in Cancún, Mexico, at the end of 2010 is the next major meeting of the UNFCCC, the first opportunity for the Peoples' Agreement to take effect in the UNFCCC process was in early June at the COP intersession held in Bonn, Germany. In terms of process, intercessional meetings are significant in as much as the outcomes tend to provide the framework for discussions at the larger COP meetings. The inclusion of the agreement in the discussions at Bonn would have been unprecedented within international negotiations; never before has a collective document of the people been submitted into a formal government negotiating process in such a manner.

However, despite the submissions of groups such as the Global Forest Coalition and other members of the CJN! network, numerous petitions, and creative protests outside the conference, calls for more stringent targets and new commitments under Kyoto were ignored. In fact not a single element of the Peoples' Agreement was included in the Bonn intercessional negotiations. Whilst this may be unsurprising given the nature of the negotiations and institutions such as the UN, it highlights the limitations of attempting to influence the UNFCCC process.

As we have argued, the UNFCCC is unwilling, and structurally incapable of, adopting positions that challenge the expansion of capitalism and the consequent deepening of ecological crises. That the People's Accord was systematically ignored serves to strengthen the argument of all those within networks such as Never Trust A COP, CJA and others that understood the COP process as serving to 'restore the legitimacy of global capitalism by inaugurating an era of "green" capitalism'. Whilst there is important work to be done resisting the worst of the policies being pushed through the UNFCCC process, it is doubtful that it can be of any use in affirming solutions to the multiple crises that we are confronting. The UNFCCC has always acted, and will continue to act, as a negotiating space for government delegations and blocs of countries protecting their individual and corporate interests, and seems completely incapable of addressing climate change or acknowledging its structural causes. Perhaps we should understand the Peoples' Agreement in this light, not as an attempt to influence the UNFCCC, but to de-legitimise it and build momentum behind an ALBA led departure from the COP process.

RADICAL DISCOURSE AND IT'S CONTRADICTIONS

Whilst the Agreement may have had no formal effect so far within the UN process, the language used has certainly contributed to the politicisation of the climate change debate. Mainstream climate change discourse has been dominated by a managerial style of 'politics without politics', which is to say that the terms of debate have been how to technically manage climate change while ignoring its structural causes. With the Reclaim Power! action at the COP15 in Copenhagen and the numerous other protests preceding it, there was arguably the emergence of a challenge to the dominance of this a-political space, an assertion that climate change is a symptom of the inherent sustainability of our economic, political and social systems. The Peoples' Agreement has re-opened the politicisation of climate change, making the contradiction between capitalism and an ecologically harmonious future explicit, as it says, 'Humanity confronts a great dilemma: to continue on the path of capitalism, depredation, and death, or to choose the path of harmony with nature and respect for life.'

The opening ceremony
of the CMPCC

This politicisation process has opened an antagonism at the heart of climate change politics, creating a division between those who maintain the possibility of ameliorating climate change through management techniques within the capitalist framework, and those who see the need for fundamental systematic change. This binary will potentially go a long way to de-legitimising the positions of many of the mainstream environmental and development NGOs engaged in the COP process, especially within the Climate Action Network (CAN). The content of the declaration will make it much harder for these NGOs pushing controversial policies, such as REDD and carbon markets, to continue claiming that they have the support of indigenous voices and social movements. Furthermore, there are indications that a rupture, drawn along the lines of this political antagonism, may well open within the UNFCCC process. Amongst a series of other aims, the delegation that presented the Peoples' Agreement to the UN indicated that they are preparing a 'demand to Annex 1 Countries that fail to comply with the Convention... to be presented if there are no substantive commitments for greenhouse gas emission reduction in Cancún'[24]. What this demand contains and how it will be presented is still unclear, but it is possible that this 'demand' will be a political move that forces states and nations to pick sides and at the same time exposes massive global inequalities.

The opening of this antagonism also fits with the broader political project of ALBA, which has been variously termed the 'pink tide' or the 'new socialism'. The antagonistic rhetoric surrounding climate change politics contributes to the drawing of a line between the ALBA project and the continuation of the neoliberal world order; as Hugo Chávez pronounced at the CMPCCC closing ceremony, paraphrasing Rosa Luxemburg: 'socialism or death'. ALBA may be in the process of positioning itself as the progressive and counter force on climate change, where the "peoples' conferences" are put in contrast to the COP meetings, and 'mother earth' is put against capitalist expansion.

Despite this rhetoric and political positioning, all of the ALBA members, Bolivia included, continue to fundamentally rely on hydrocarbons for their social programmes and development. Eduardo Gudynas has understood this reliance on hydrocarbons and other extractive industries as a 'new extractivism that maintains a style of development based on the appropriation of Nature.'[25] As has been suggested in the earlier discussion about the relations between capitalism and climate change, the radical anti-capitalist rhetoric of ALBA has yet to manifest itself in a concrete change in conditions based on an ecological sensibility. This new extractivism may well provide the basis for an increase in social welfare for large parts of these countries' populations, and this has its benefits. However, it does not in practice challenge the premise of capitalist models of development. As such, whilst the rhetoric of these states may be attractive in comparison to the perpetuation of neoliberal false solutions, the creation of viable alternatives has been slow or non-existent. Whilst this is a common factor with some other anti-capitalist politics, it reminds us of the need for a completely different relationship between resources, the state and the population.

<24> http://motherearthrights.org/2010/05/07/actions-agreed-upon-during-the-meeting-of-the-delegation-that-presented-the-conclusions-of-the-cmpcc-at-the-un/

<25> Gudynas, E. (2010) 'The New Extractavism of the 21st Century: Ten Urgent Theses about Extractavism in Relation to Current South American Progressivism', Americas Program Report, January 21, 2010

The conference may have brought some much-needed international attention to the struggles people are facing in the global south and specifically in Bolivia, with the protests in San Cristóbal being no coincidence (box v). It has also greatly impacted on the awareness and understanding of climate change in Bolivia, with changing weather patterns and melting glaciers increasingly being understood as part of much larger changes occurring in Earth's climate. In addition the CMPCC, through mobilising social movements, has reinvigorated debate in peoples' networks and specifically in Bolivia, where further attention was drawn to some of the contradictions between the actions and words of the government. The People's agreement may also assist social movements by acting as a tool to hold the government to account over its commitments. What spaces like the Mesa 18 reminded us is that rhetoric is not enough to deal with the problems we face, and that whilst the CMPCC may have progressed debate, we need to go much further than make proclamations if we are to create new, ecologically harmonious ways of organising our societies. In considering how to use the Peoples Agreement and how to participate in future events similar to the CMPCC we need consider the implications of engaging in such politics that push us out of our comfort zones, but also the implications of not doing so; we need to take into account the full range of dangers and potentials of such interactions between states and movements.

Evo Morales speech at the closing ceremony of the CMPCC

Mural from the Red Tinku social centre, Cochabamba

9.

QUE COMPLICADO! — CLOSING REFLECTIONS

It is now time to try and pull together some of our diverse thoughts. We will reflect on some of the difficult questions that we are left with, which others may also wish consider. We are not intending to provide definitive answers, but instead share some of our thinking and reflections. As the title of this section suggests – it is complicated, a recurrent feeling we all shared throughout this whole project, in which we tried to look at the grey areas rather than coming down clearly on one side of an argument.

The climate crisis has been presented and discussed within the official negotiations as a technocratic, apolitical issue – this is to say, they reduce the cause of climate change to simply an issue of the concen-

1. IS CLIMATE CHANGE A TERRAIN OF STRUGGLE?

tration of greenhouse gases in the atmosphere, mainly from industries. Therefore, responses such as carbon markets or 'technofixes' like Carbon Capture and Storage[26], are the only cards on the intergovernmental table. On the other hand we are told by liberal NGOs and governments that it is 'us,' our individual energy consumption, that is the problem – that

if only we used energy-efficient light bulbs, recycled our waste, or all went vegan, we could each 'play our part' in solving the crisis. Additionally, groups such as the Optimum Population Trust[27] further detract attention from the real causes by encouraging carbon offsetting through population controls.

It is evident that none of these responses acknowledge let alone tackle the systemic causes of the problems that we face. Climate change becomes a political issue when we question the reasons behind the domination of these industries, when we look at who are profiting from these false solutions and who are being dispossessed, when we oppose the value of profit and hegemonic aim of economic growth, when we challenge the social relations which have got us into this mess. We argue that a political and radical approach entails understanding the power dynamics that have caused and are accelerating the crisis, recognizing that climate change is a consequence of our political and economic systems and that addressing it means fighting for systemic changes.

<26> See Corporate Watch's 'Technofix Report': corporatewatch.org.uk/?lid=3126

<27> See Pop Offsets: popoffsets.com

Rather than isolating climate change as an issue to campaign 'against', it must be understood as the most devastating symptom of the way our societies are organised. In which case, the task of overcoming climate change becomes the even more daunting task of reorganising our societies. In addressing how we do this, everything comes into play; from the division of people by class, nationality or gender, the lack of access to food and shelter, or the prevalence of mental health issues in 'developed' nations. For example, we see that a key tool of the capitalist system that lies at the root of the problem is the division of human beings into distinct categories and nationalities. States who are competing economically will never be able to reach a consensus on how to deal with climate change, and this logic of borders and nationalism leads governments to construct walls and militarise borders in response to anticipated displacement through climate change and all its myriad impacts. It is this logic that allows countries to trade their emissions while people are forced off their lands. It is this logic that leads to wars over dwindling fossil fuel resources. These borders are also an attempt to stop us realising our common humanity. But there are many people struggling to overcome these arbitrary divisions. Acting in solidarity together across deserts, fences and seas and struggling for freedom of movement for all has been and will continue to be a central terrain of struggle for many.

Recognising the many related struggles that each respond according to their angle of analyses can lead us towards a complete transformation in the way we conceptualise the problem of climate change and therefore to a more holistic and political approach. For this reason, there is no issue that fails to have implications for tackling climate change, and any attempt to separate it as an issue distinct from these struggles is senseless. Despite the progress that has been made in this area over the past few years, there remains an enormous amount of work to do here, and this remains a fundamental struggle.

2. WHERE NOW FOR CLIMATE JUSTICE?

Climate justice is a contested term, and questions remain over how, or indeed whether, it can help quite disparate struggles to unite into wider movements. It is important not to romanticise the concept as inherently radical nor assume that it always comes directly from people on the frontline of struggle. We must be conscious of how and why we are using the term in our discourse and actions, and what are the limits to this.

Many organisations, such as the Durban Group for Climate Justice and those in CJN!, have been crucial in raising popular awareness and resisting the creation and implementation of carbon markets and false solutions inside, and outside, the COP process. Meanwhile others, such as Rising Tide and CJA, have helped to open up the space for furthering a systemic critique of climate change and mobilising people to take direct action against the root causes. It is clear, however, that much more work is required if climate justice is to become an effective concept for linking up and expanding the social struggles we desperately require in the face of numerous crises.

Rather than just asking what climate justice is – to which there are many answers – we need to begin to ask what climate justice can do. Does using this term bring us closer to achieving things we would otherwise fail to? Perhaps, at the very least, it can help us to move beyond ideas that climate change is somehow separate from the rest of our lives. More importantly, it can be used to re-politicise the crisis in a way that refocuses attention back on the way our societies are organised and move us beyond the illusion that a few wind-turbines topped with a dose of austerity can solve what is a systemic problem.

However, this can only be done by opposing the more problematic and contradictory uses of the term. How and where are calls for 'climate justice' being interpreted as mere monetary, legal or regulatory solutions, and how do we challenge this recuperation without walking away from the concept altogether? This also opens up uncomfortable questions about who can own an idea and who has the ability to define it.

The concept of climate justice can also contribute to an ecological critique of capitalism, understanding how the processes of endless accumulation are in contradiction with the planet's biophysical limits. Capitalism, for the sake of profit, captures and exploits not only our human capacities, but the basic conditions of existence itself. As the saying goes, "you can't have infinite growth on a finite planet." In a move beyond Hugo Chavez's formulation, we are confronted not with 'socialism or death', but 'capitalism or life'.

This is perhaps the point when the perspective of climate justice really can begin to do something. A life without capitalism is not an absence, it is life – indeed this life comes before and in spite of capitalism. The very reason we face these multiple crises is the single, hegemonic, value of capital – profitability. For us to be able to make free decisions about how we meet our needs and desires while living in ecological balance, it is essential that there are many worlds imagined without capitalism, many different values around which we can organise our lives. As Soumitra Ghosh says, 'the neo-liberal ONE must be opposed with our local MANY; the hegemony of capital needs to be countered with our diverse plurality.'

Climate justice, then, can be part of opening up these many answers, of developing many strategies that suit the conditions of where they are developed. This is where climate justice can help us to find resonance – in its ability to bring people into an antagonistic relation with capital, but more importantly, doing so through the active creation of different ways of organising existence. Perhaps it is this conception of climate justice, as the creation of harmonious ways of living, that brings us closest to understanding the Andean indigenous concept of Buen Vivir, translating more or less as 'to live well';

"Buen Vivir is a solid principle which means life in harmony and equilibrium between men and women, between different communities and, above all, between human beings and the natural environment of which they are part. In practice, this concept implies knowing how to live in community with others while achieving a minimum degree of equality. It means eliminating prejudice and exploitation between people as well as respecting nature and preserving its equilibrium".[28]

<28> indybay.org/newsitems/2010/02/28/18... – The original article "Sumac Kawsay" was published on the Web site of Foro Social Mundial on 6 February 2009. The Spanish translation by Blanca Diego, "Buen Vivir," was published on the same site on the same day. English translation by Christopher Reid.

The crisis of climate change is by all accounts an urgent one. Numerous reports have been released detailing the dangerous potential of 'feedback mechanisms', where the direct impacts of climate change,

3. HOW CAN WE DEAL WITH SHORT-TERM NEEDS AND LONG-TERM CHANGE AT THE SAME TIME?

such as desertification, lead to further carbon emissions that then trigger further effects. To avoid the worst effects, we are told, we have to peak global carbon emissions in a number of years rather than decades, and then pursue a rapid decrease in the years after. Whilst this science is by no means a perfect art, it is clear we are facing a very real and urgent threat that requires immediate action.

Whilst we must not ignore the urgency of the situation, this timescale has resulted in a tendency to accept 'any deal' or 'any initiative' that claims it will address the problem. This way, any form of systemic critique or radical assessment of how we are going to escape from this crisis is negated and repressed. In this framework climate justice becomes either co-opted as a manipulative tool by groups such as TckTckTck, or is sidelined altogether. The political capitulation to urgency also detours leads us back to a technocratic assessment of the problem, where our choices are either to join the calls for 'green capitalism' and technofixes, or to pursue the perverse concept of 'rioting for austerity'.

The call for austerity is politically implausible as it relies on the opposition between human well-being and ecological well-being, where austerity ultimately means accepting a miserable life in the name of saving the planet. A mandate for rule based on reducing carbon emissions at the expense of all other struggles would lead to a kind of 'green authoritarianism' fundamentally opposed to the collectively free societies that we desire, supporting the expansion of social controls and market logic under the guise of protecting us against climate change. This position is one we should categorically reject; we are calling for a world of human and ecological betterment, the two are not opposed.

When considering how the mainstream environmental movement has dealt with the issue of achieving short-term changes, it is obvious that concessions have been made far too easily. The approach to urgency and the possibility of achieving results in terms of government policy have all too often led to capitulation and watering down of demands. Even if much harder positions were adopted, the reliance on lobbying of governments will not address the fundamental structural causes of the problem, and in many cases leads to policies that reinforce the systems that are at the root of the current crises.

On the other hand, just as the need for urgent action on climate change has led some to ignore its structural causes, many of those who have a more systemic critique are prone to ignore the issue of how to achieve rapid reductions in emissions. Neither perspective brings us any closer to a realistic strategy. So the question remains as to how existing institutions and structures can be forced to make immediate changes to the way we produce and distribute energy, the way we grow and distribute our food, the way we house ourselves and keep ourselves healthy? Crucially, can we force these institutions to make these changes without compromising the rise of a generalised movement for a better world, without compromising or losing site of our ultimate aims?

However an individual or group responds to this this question it is clear that concentrating solely on immediate emissions reductions and ignoring the historical causes or future, albeit unintended, consequences could be disastrous. There may well be strategic moments where we can successfully intervene to prevent the exploitation of tar sands or new coal fields – we should find these moments, and act on them! Yet at the same time we must also explore how we create our other worlds, how we organise our societies in a way that provides for our needs and desires, without pitting ourselves against ecological harmony. And we must do this now.

Despite all of our criticisms of an emissions-centric world view there is important work to be done in resisting the exploration and extraction of fossil fuels and rapidly reducing our reliance on them. Our local resilience as communities is fundamentally important and, as long as it is carried out alongside resisting capitalism and social control, is an important part of solidarity. Connecting struggles around fossil fuels and false solutions to climate change – from industrial pollution and monoculture plantations to financial accumulation, is also key.

4. ACROSS INTERNATIONAL AND CLASS DIVIDES: HOW DO WE WORK IN SOLIDARITY AS EQUALS?

Although the politics of solidarity have been widely discussed among movements, often, but certainly not always, much of this has remained as rhetoric. We have learned that in order to engage with each other as equals it is equally important to neither idealise nor to patronise other struggles. Whilst the form of any struggle depends on its local context, in many cases we can see that we are fighting on different terrains toward the same broad goals. But to take it a step further, what does it really mean to relate as equals while respecting our diversities? How can we understand each other from the outside when we are unaware of the complex nuances that other social movements may be dealing with?

Just as capitalist relations and the operations of transnational corporations continue to spread around the globe, so our resistance must also surpass geographic boundaries. In this, we should not assume shared values or impose agendas, but engage in dialogue, recognise each other's messy politics and look for the possible connections. This will be a continual learning process, but it is one that we must have if we are to deal with the challenges that exist outside of our individual localities. Sharing skills, knowledge and experiences, researching and uncovering links between our local situations and jointly targeting and building up personal trust between individuals are a few potential examples here. It will involve continually improving our awareness of situations in other parts of the world and in other realities on our own doorsteps. Communication with others and reflection on our own actions, agendas and solidarities is vital whether it be between neighbouring communities or across regions and continents.

But these exchanges can expose different values and ways of working and will require dialogue and sensitivity. A highly undesirable outcome would be to force an agenda, or assume an affinity, as this can unintentionally lead to further division and distrust. In looking to connect struggles, we need to break down false hierarchies and constantly reflect on our joint and collective agendas. As we move collectively towards our other worlds, and as we strive to make decisions based on values other than profit, we must understand that the values of others are not always necessarily exactly the same as ours. These are the real challenges of building and strengthening effective global movements. Solidarity, like any relationship, brings its own tensions, power relations and politics to be recognised and dealt with. Solidarity means finding ways to resonate together – not imposing any value or dominant framework for engaging with the world. In practice, this means not rejecting this or that struggle because it does not fit exactly with our own ideological framework – as some have done in reaction to the CMPCC; It means not hiding behind ourselves and resting in our comfortable niches; It means reflecting on our own politics and relations both locally and beyond boundaries, but always walking the line between our dreams and reality.

5. WHAT CAN BE LEARNED FROM THE MESSY POLITICS OF SOCIAL MOVEMENTS INTERACTING WITH STATES?

Just as governments and corporations can't deal with climate change, it is also important to realise the complexities and limitations of social movements. We don't want to conclude in a way that suggests any easy binaries. Frequently used terms such as 'social movements' or 'state' mean different things and provoke different reactions in different contexts. With the complex interplay of relations, it is necessary to escape from simplifications. By airing some of the debates around the CMPCC, the aim is not to say that we would necessarily do any better, or that it is possible or desirable to achieve a pure political space free from contradictions. The space for movement is perhaps within our own understandings of where we want to be going with our political organising and how we get there.

We are left with the question of how movements based in Europe and other parts of the world can interact with movements in Latin America and elsewhere who are themselves engaged in the messy politics of relations with the state. In some cases this needs to be considered in a context where presidents who do not comply with the people's agendas are frequently overthrown.

For centuries now in Bolivia and Latin America, movements are constantly re-shaping and re-articulating spaces and politics. As the Uruguayan Raúl Zibechi said, "It is no longer about social movements but about entire societies that have started to move"[29]. In countries where the classic divisions between the people and the state are now blurring, and new actors and agendas have started to re-articulate these spaces. Bolivia helped us to understand how it is not a simple choice between movements either keeping their 'radical position' or taking state power: rather, it is about powerful grassroots collectivities bringing change from below. Although instinctively we tend to reject any interaction with the state, looking at all the layers and resistances that underlie this moment provokes and requires a more careful and considered response. Within inspiring examples of social change there are always internal contradictions and cracks to explore. They are fascinating and reveal some of the most complex discussions.

If strong social movements were to emerge in Europe then similar antagonisms would inevitably appear. We cannot pretend that they will not exist nor merely dismiss all those with whom we have differences of opinion. Instead we must continue to search for the fruitful common ground. There must always be room to manoeuvre, openness to dissent and critique, and a rejection of dogma and staleness. As we, rightly, criticise hierarchy and top-down organising

<29> Zibechi, R. (2007) "Autonomías y emancipaciones. América Latina en movimiento". Colección Transformación Global.

we must always ask ourselves how successful non-hierarchical groups are and how they can be improved. How can we learn from our mistakes? While we are certainly not calling for a European-wide creation of progressive political parties nor support for those that may already exist, we must be realistic about what our goals are and how we achieve them, both in the short and long term. In this way, we must also be open in our assessments of the successes and failures of political movements that differ dramatically from our own.

A look at any Indymedia page from across Europe reveals some of the political organising happening around a city and tells us about some of the diverse struggles; Various anti-deportation campaigns to

6. HOW DOES IT RELATE TO OUR DAILY STRUGGLES?

resist the racist immigration regime, community projects against gang culture, resisting cuts to public services, occupation of abandoned buildings as free spaces, permaculture gardens, recycling food that would otherwise go to waste to create shared meals, mobilising for a No Border camp in Brussels (the seat of European government), supporting those on trial for smashing up an arms factory in protest at the bombing of Gaza, a bike ride to raise awareness of struggles against fossil fuel expansion, forming an alliance of those in debt, disseminating and producing independent media, films and radio...the list goes on.

There is no shortage of things for us to do, to take action on, to organise around, to mobilise for, to act in solidarity with. But how do all these things link up into effective movements that can change the relationships that our current form of social organisation is founded upon? What is the longer term strategy to link up these moments into a real force for social change? How can we ensure we maintain our diversity when strategising, allowing autonomous individuals and groups to act at their chosen point and with their chosen method of intervention, whilst still moving towards actual change?

Many activists seem to chose their path by where they can see the results most clearly, or are constantly busy responding to the latest crisis. The hard work of longer term strategy or building movements can often be neglected. Especially once the common enemy is taken out of the equation the challenge of moving beyond single issue campaigns or summit mobilisations becomes clear. What unites us on a deeper level? How can we become solid enough to withstand repression and internal divisions? Rather than waiting for some magic catalysing moment, we need to create and use common spaces to strategise and discuss together, to talk about where it is we are actually going and how we might eventually get there. Clear answers will not easily be found and there will be disagreements, complications and hurdles. We need to find time to have the fundamental conversations about how social change happens. Constantly questioning, re-debating and opening these spaces for movement may be our best chance.

To weave together our disparate struggles we must foster dignity and mutual respect. Laying good foundations for working together is fundamental to resisting the alienation and competition that we are socialised into. As we critically analyse each other it is important to consider that while some may have a personal or ideological reason for rejecting something, others may have a very good reason for not doing so. Communication and contextualisation are key.

Perhaps the most important question raised by the CMPCC and its Bolivian context was concerning the nature of allies – who or what can we find allegiance with? This is a question that goes far beyond an issue of specific movement politics to the very basis of how we conceive of change; for this reason, it is also perhaps the most tentative of contributions.

Our fears and concerns about this conference, especially regarding our engagement with processes of the state, were informed both by experience and ideology. Returning from Bolivia, we are no closer to providing a definitive answer that vindicates either our ideological opposition to the state or the 'actually existing' experiences in Bolivia. Perhaps this is because these two tendencies – being opposed to the state or engaging with the state – are not necessarily as contradictory as the 'horizontalism / verticalism' divide of the past 15 years would have it.

We must come to understand the actions of ourselves and others not on ideology alone, on principles that we separate from the world, but on a politics of how the world actually unfolds. The world we live in contains both the social relations that we bitterly oppose – the state and capitalism to name but a few – and our ideologies, our dreams of a different way of organising our lives. These dreams are just as real as those social relations we are opposed to; they are not confined merely to the inactivity of our sleep.

The point is for us to realise that these ideologies, these dreams, are just one factor among many. We must not elevate these ideas of a future without capitalism, exploitation and hierarchy into a heaven outside of this world, believing that we are some kind of superior beings in the process. This places them in an immortal place that cannot be touched, abstracts that are nothing more than make-believe.

Instead, what happens when we embed our dreams in this world? This entails playing out our ideologies alongside everything else in this world, understanding that they are both ends and means at the same time. This means embarking on a journey from the way things currently exist and moving towards worlds we want to be in, but always rooting this in the present. This doesn't mean giving up on our desires, nor does it mean living a contradiction. It means accepting that our ideologies are a part of reality, that we can never live according to dreams alone, but that our challenge is to make them work alongside and in conjunction with the rest of the world.

At times everyone feels overwhelmed by the scale of the problems and the challenges we face. What has inspired us is to have met so many different people who really believe in their collective power to change things. There is undoubtedly much to learn from how this was achieved and from these ongoing stories. Back home, wherever that may be, we need to sow these seeds of determination, to help them spread in whatever ways we can.

As we reflect back to the mural on the cover of this text, we picture our diverse experiences, histories and futures continuing to weave together into powerful moments of social change. Imagining a future free from domination and exploitation that respects and creates space for the multiplicities of our experiences, locations, needs and desires, whilst bringing us together, ready for the challenges we continue to face. These pages will hopefully contribute to some of the ongoing discussions in different places around the world, as each of us take our next steps.

xi.

ON OCTOBER 12, 2010: CHANGE THE SYSTEM, NOT THE CLIMATE!

Call for a global day of direct action for climate justice

The disaster that was the climate summit in Copenhagen highlighted one thing above all: that we cannot expect UN-negotiations to solve the climate crisis for us. Governments and corporations are unable (even if they were willing) to deliver real climate justice. Only powerful, global climate justice movements can achieve the structural changes that are necessary, whether it is ending our addiction to fossil fuels, replacing industrial agriculture with local systems of food sovereignty, halting systems based on endless growth and consumption, or addressing the historical responsibility of the global elites' massive ecological debt to the global exploited.

The Latin American network 'Global Minga' called for an annual day of action in defence of mother earth on October 12, reclaiming the day that used to be imposed as 'Columbus Day'. Responding to this call, and the demand for a day of action for 'system change, not climate change' made in Copenhagen by global movements, Climate Justice Action is proposing a day of direct action for climate justice on October 12, 2010.

We invite all those who fight for social and ecological justice to organise direct actions targeting climate criminals and false solutions, or creating real alternatives. This is an open callout, we are not picking targets. But it is not a day for marches or petitions: it is time for us to reclaim our power, and take control of our lives and futures.

xii.

A THOUSAND CANCUNS! VIA CAMPESINA – FACING THE COP16

1. The capitalist model that prioritises benefits for transnational corporations over those of the people and respect for nature is driving us towards the destruction of our planet. Transnational corporations are our common enemies, they are enemies of humanity.

The future of humanity is under threat. Industrial agriculture and livestock and the commercialised food system, along with the atmospheric contamination caused by these large industries, are what is provoking the climate crisis. The life, knowledge and culture of peasant and indigenous communities are at risk, and with them sufficient and healthy food production are at risk as well.

2. La Vía Campesina's struggle is a different approach, which values and protects the knowledge, culture and role of peasant and indigenous small producers and family farms in food production. We are the solution to hunger in the world and our agriculture cools the planet.

Food sovereignty is the global alternative confronting the capitalist system and the multidimensional crisis it has generated (food crisis, biodiversity crisis, financial crisis, energy crisis), it is an alternative for society as a whole.

3. After the failure of the United Nations Conference of the Parties on Climate Change in Copenhagen (COP 15), the COP 16 will be held in Cancun, Mexico from November 29th to December 10th, 2010. We do not doubt that the governments of the dominant countries, and their loyal allies in the South, are planning to meet again to continue profiting on the basis of false solutions – such as agrofuels and the carbon credits market – rather than addressing the real structural causes of the climate crisis, which is part of the current multifaceted crisis of capitalism.

4. We are in high spirits following the World People's Conference on Climate Change and the Rights of Mother Earth, which took place in Cochabamba, Bolivia this past April. The agreements affirm the rights of peasant and indigenous peoples, as well as the rights of Mother Earth herself, and demand that industrialised countries assume their historical responsibility for the climate crisis with real and drastic emissions cuts and the payment of their climate debt, among other things.

Cancun, Mexico will be a distinct field of battle from the one in which we derailed the WTO in 2003. So, we have made a call to create "Thousands of Cancuns" throughout the world and throughout Mexico, during the dates when the COP 16 will take place, in which we, the people, will show our complete disagreement with the false solutions of big capital and bad governments and our firm determination to struggle for the real solutions. We are calling for a process of struggle in which the basis will be the political positioning regarding the subject and the real alternatives.

In Cancun, La Vía Campesina and allies will construct an Alternative Forum and we will mobilise to create a "sounding board" that will be heard and repeated in the many other "Cancuns" that will take place. The task is to create many Cancuns so that the real reason and the real promise of the struggle will spread throughout the entire world.

We propose starting now to impulse a process of constructing spaces and real articulations from organizations and social movements, and that we meet again leading up to August with constructed processes, from local and regional levels, to evaluate and consolidate the thousands of Cancuns. Today there are a number of initiatives proposed leading up to the COP 16, but none of them represent us. In particular, La Vía Campesina distances itself from certain "self convened" groups, and those who say they speak on behalf of social movements but who in reality are protagonists for their NGO. We want to construct processes and spaces so that more non-comformist voices can express their struggles. It is necessary to articulate, inform, organise and in this way from our struggles, from our bases, build a large world movement for Mother Earth.

We are for a real process of constructing spaces from the movements from below, along with goodhearted allies throughout the world and Mexico.

Peasants cool down the planet.
Globalise the struggle. Globalise hope!!!

GLOSSARY

This is a guide to some of the acronyms and key words used in this booklet. We are not attempting to provide objective definitions, just attempting to give the reader a better understanding by introducing some the terms we use.

ACRONYMS

ALBA = Bolivarian Alliance for the Americas

ALBA-TCP = Peoples Trade Treaty

CAFTA = Central America Free Trade Agreement

CAN = Climate Action Network

CJA = Climate Justice Action

CJN! = Climate Justice Now!

CMPCC/WPCCC = Conferencia Mundial de los Pueblos sobre el Cambio Climático y los Derechos de la Madre Tierra/World Peoples Conference on Climate Change and the Rights of Mother Earth

CMS = Consejo de Movimientos Sociales (Social Movements Council)

CO3 = Bolivian Workers Union

COMIBOL = Bolivian state-owned mining company

CONAMAQ = National Council of Ayllus and Markas of the Qullasuyu

COP = Conference of Parties

CSUTCB = Confederación Sindical Única de Trabajadores Campesinos de Bolivia (merger of several peasants union)

EU ETS = European Union Emissions Trading Scheme

EZLN = Ejército Zapatista de Liberación Nacional (The Zapatista Army of National Liberation)

FTAA = Free Trade Area of the Americas

IMF = International Monetary Fund

IOM = International Organisation for Migration

MAS = Partido Movimiento al Socialismo (Movement towards Socialism party)

MNR = Nationalist Revolutionary Movement Party

MST = Movimento dos Trabalhadores Rurais Sem Terra (Brazil's Landless Workers Movement)

NAFTA = The North American Free Trade Agreement

NGO = Non Governmental Organisation

NTAC = Never Trust A COP

REDD = Reduced Emissions through Deforestation and Degradation

SEMAPA = Bolivian state utility company

UNASUR = Unión Sudamericana de Naciones (South American Nations Unity)

UNFCCC = United Nations Framework Convention on Climate Change

USSR = Union of Soviet Socialist Republics

Via Campesina = international peasants movement (defending the values and basic interests of peasants, small- and medium-sized producers, landless, rural women, indigenous people, rural youth and agricultural workers)

WB = World Bank

KEY WORDS

Bottom-up = A term used in organisational or systems theory that means the opposite of top-down hierarchical organisation. We understand that it is relevant to building movements led by those who are the worst off in any given society.

Chicago Boys = A group of Chilean economists trained in Chicago under the neoliberal guru Milton Friedman. Many became key advisers to the Pinochet dictatorship, which implemented savaged neoliberal reforms.

Colonialism = The invasion and maintaining of 'colonies' in occupied territories by people based elsewhere. Understood as the historical period from the 15th to the 20th century when political and economic elites in Europe established colonies on other continents.

The Common = Refers to the dynamic entirety of life. It is the air, the water, the fruits of the soil, and all nature's bounty but also and more significantly those results of social production that are necessary for social interaction and further production, such as knowledge, languages, codes, information. We, 'the subject', are therefore coproduced as part of the common.

The commons = Resources that are collectively owned or shared between or among populations, as opposed to private property. Usually refers to elements of the natural environment.

Communism = In orthodox Marxist theory, communism is a situation in which society is self-managed by the free association of individuals. This point of free association of individuals is also what many anarchists aspire to achieve. The term has been largely discredited due to its misuse by the oppressive socialist states that dominated the 20th century, but is nonetheless an important concept in political theory.

Constituent Assembly of Bolivia = An assembly formed in 2006 with the aim of writing a new national constitution that would redress historical oppression of Indigenous Peoples. It was a controversial process that was opposed by the majority of the conservative population, mostly white, European descendants or mestizo. After years of legal wrangling, a referendum and mass demonstrations and rallies the new constitution finally passed in February 2009.

Country = Any geopolitical organisation of a landmass and the people contained within it.

Coup d'état = The overthrow of a government by a group from within the institutions of the state, usually the military, or from outside the state.

Decolonisation = The process by which a formerly colonised country attempts to reverse the impacts of colonialism. Often used regarding only material distribution, however, also understood as the imposed cultures, mentalities and political ideologies. A decolonisation process involves a holistic transformation of the colonialist structures.

Free Trade = A key tenet of neoliberalism, 'free trade' is the idea that capital (ie. money) and goods should be able to move freely without state intervention. Those that support the idea of 'free trade' are therefore opposed to trade tariffs, and often taxation.

G77 = The Group of 77 at the United Nations is a loose coalition of 'developing' nations. There are now more than 130 nations in the G77.

Gas Wars = The Bolivian peoples' conflict against gas privatisation, beginning in 2003. Also a key struggle in fomenting the resistance which ultimately led to the election of Evo Morales.

Greenwash = The practice of companies' deceptive use of green marketing to make the public believe that they are adopting practices beneficial to the environment when in reality they do nothing.

Imperialism = The creation, maintenance and imposition of an unequal economic, cultural, political and territorial relationship, usually between states and often in the form of an empire, based on domination and subordination.

Keynesian = Economic theory based on ideas of 20th century economist John M. Keynes. Promotes predominantly private sector economies, but with significant governmental/public control of economic activities.

Multinational = A multinational corporation (MNC) is a corporation with extensive ties in international operations in more than one foreign country.

Nation = A concept, probably emerging at the time of the French revolution, which claims there exists a set of values which holds specific people together. It was created to legitimise the rule of the state; the 'nation' can be understood to have a 'general will' which can be 'represented' by a government.

Nation-state = A nation-state is any state which directly derives its legitimacy from representing a single nation. Often associated with the concept of a nations right to self-determination.

Neocolonialism = A new form of colonialism where governments and corporations continue occupying territotries to exploit people and resources of, and exert economic control over post-colonial states. Can also refer to wealthy nations exerting control to other nations' values and perceptions through cultural means, such as media, language, education and religion.

Neoliberalism = A set of policies under an specific era of capitalism, arguably beginning with the election of Thatcher (UK) in 1979 and Reagan (US) in 1981. The key tenet is that unfettered capitalism, with no state interference, is the most effective way to organise society. The neoliberal 'project' led to mass privatisation of public services, and transformed the Bretton Woods institutions (WB, IMF, and later the WTO) into international organisations for the furthering of neoliberal policies.

Progressive = A term that almost exclusively relies upon who is using it. In general, something described as 'progressive' will theoretically move us towards a more equitable and just society.

Proxy War = A proxy war is a war fought between two powers in a third party country. This was common during the Cold War, when the USSR and the West never had a direct war, but instead heavily backed 'socialist' or 'capitalist' factions in countries such as Korea or Vietnam.

Reformism = A belief that the dominant structures in the world, such as the state and capitalism, can be mediated through implementing policies. Reformism is often contrasted with revolution, which suggests a better life is ultimately only possible through the overthrowing of the state and capitalism.

Socialism = In orthodox Marxist theory, socialism is the necessary step between capitalism and communism, where the proletariat takes control of the state to establish the 'dictatorship of the proletariat'. This enables the management of resources and social relations in the interest of fostering the 'free association' of peoples – communism – before the state then dissolves itself. In actuality socialism is often used incorrectly, often as a replacement for communism in an attempt to distance oneself from the miserable history of the 20th century.

Social Movement = A contested term under constant redefinition. It is generally used to refer to a series of non-state actors, all of which are contesting a series of struggles that are in some way interconnected. Examples could be the gay rights movement, civil rights movement, or alter-globalisation 'movement of movements'.

Social Relations = Relationships between people, including their behaviour, actions, gestures and desires towards each other. Under capitalism, these relationships become relationships of domination and exploitation where people are forced to sell their labour and work for others in order to survive.

State = 'The state', as used in this text, is the set of institutions that make and enforce the rules that govern people in one or more societies.

Territories = A term within political geography, referring to any area of land under the control of a certain government. Indigenous Peoples use the word 'territories' to associate their lands to the all their necessary attributes (medicines, shelter, food, etc).

Transnational = A Transnational Corporation is a MNC that operates worldwide without being identified with a national home base. It is said to operate on a border less basis.

Washington Consensus = Synonymous with neoliberalism, the Washington Consensus was a package of policies imposed to many 'developing' countries for the expansion of neoliberal economic policies.

Water Wars = The Bolivian peoples' conflict against international water consortium Aguas de Tunari, beginning in 2000. Sometimes used to refer to the ongoing struggles for water in Bolivia. The water wars were a key struggle in fomenting the resistance which ultimately led to the election of Evo Morales.

RECOMMENDED FURTHER READING:

Benjamin Dangl (2009) El Precio del Fuego, Plural Editores, Bolivia.

Benjamin Dangl, (2007) The Price of Fire, Resource Wars and Social Movements in Bolivia. AK Press.

Raúl Zibechi (2007), 'Autonomías y emancipaciones. América Latina en movimiento'. Programa Democracia y TRansformación Global y UNMSM, Perú.

Raphael Hoetmer (2009), 'Repensar la política desde América Latina'. Programa Democracia y Transformación Global y UNMSM, Perú.

Oscar Olivera, Raquel Gutiérrez, Marcela Olivera, Tom Lewis (2008), 'Nosotros somos la Coordinadora'. Fundación Abril/textos rebeldes, Bolivia.

Oscar Olivera & Tom Lewis (2004) '¡Cochabamba! Water War in Bolivia' South End Press

Eduardo Galeano (1971), 'Open Veins of Latin America: Five Centuries of the Pillage of a Continent'.

Tamra Gilbertson and Oscar Reyes, Carbon Trading- What it is and Why it Fails, , Critical Currents no. 7, November 2009

Why Climate Change is not an environmental Issue? pamphlet, Available on the Web: http://notenvironmental.blogspot.com/

FOR MORE INFORMATION ON RECENT ANTI-CAPITALIST, ENVIRONMENTAL AND CLIMATE CHANGE RELATED STRUGGLES IN EUROPE:

Harvie, D; Milburn, K; Trott, B; Watts, D. (2005) Shut Them Down, Leeds: Dissent!

Notes from Nowhere (2003) We Are Everywhere, London: Verso

Wall, D. (1999) Earth First and the Anti-roads Movement: Radical Environmentalism and Comparative Social Movements, London: Routledge

Pusey, A. & Russell, B. (2010) 'The Climate Crisis or the Crisis of Climate Politics', Anarchist Studies 2010, Available on the Web: anarchiststudies.org/node/423

Anonymous (2009) Dealing with Distractions, Available on the Web: i.ixnp.com/images/v6.35/t.gif

Do or Die: Voices from Ecological Resistance (UK, 1992-2003): eco-action.org/dod

Trapese Collective , Do It Yourself, A Handbook for Changing our World, Pluto Press, 2007, www.trapese.org

'Castor' Anti-Nuclear protests   http:// thecommune.wordpress.com/2009/06/13/nuclear-waste-transport-protests-in-germany-we-shall-be-in-the-way

UK Camp for Climate Action: climatecamp.org.uk

French Camp Action Climat: campclimat.org

Nordic Camp for Climate Action: nordiccamp.org

Climate Justice Action: climate-justice-action.org

No Border Network: noborder.org

An A-Z of Borders, Perspectives from the No Border Network, http://wiki.noborders.org.uk/workspace/A-_Z_workspace

BIOGRAPHIES

Thank-you to all these people and we hope that we have translated and used your comments as they were intended.

1. **Nick Buxton** is the online communications and media officer at the Transnational Institute (TNI), and worked as the media officer for the CMPCCC and the Bolivian delegation at COP-15. He previously lived in Bolivia for four years, working as writer/web editor at Fundación Solón, a Bolivian organisation working on issues of trade, water, culture and historical memory. He is long-term active on global justice and peace issues. In the late 1990s he was communications manager at Jubilee 2000, part of the global movement that put unjust international debt on the global political agenda. We met him through contacts and whilst at the conference.

2. **Carlos Crespo Flores** is a sociologist at the Universidad Mayor de San Simon, Cochabamba. He co-ordinates the environmental work of the Centre for Higher University Studies, (CESU) and works in the areas of ecology and politics of water, racism and urban segregation. He is part of a network for the development of water in Bolivia, CGIAB (*Comision para la gestion integral del agua en Bolivia*) that was briefly part of the newly created Ministry of Water. He was also involved in the creation of Mesa 18.
We were recommended to speak to him by Marcela Olivera.

3. **Jimmy Cruz** works in communication for PROBIOMA (*Productividad Biosfera and Medio Ambiente* www.probioma.org.bo) PROBIOMA is focused on productivity, environment and sustainability in Santa Cruz, Bolivia. We met him at Mesa 18, where PROBIOMA highlighted the water war commemorations and also had a stall outside Mesa 18.

4. **Alejandra Escobar** is a student of Pedagogy living in Cochabamba, Bolivia. She identifies with the Quechua people and is a city-based indigenous activist. She has worked with Somos Sur (We are the South), a foundation focused on popular education and communication to strengthen and "support the process of change" in Bolivia. Alejandra also hosts a daily radio program called Rebelde (Rebel), with activist orientated themes from a indigenous perspective. We met her through living in Cochabamba and she was Spanish teacher to two of us.

5. **Florine Quispe Flores** comes from the Poopó province in the Oruro department, Bolivia. He is considered a native authority in this area as he is the general secretary of CORIDU (Coordinating Organization for the Defense of the Poopó and Uru Uru lakes and the Desaguadero river)
We met him during the discussions at the Mesa 18.

6. **Fabricio Guamán** lives in Quito, Ecuador and has been working for several years with indigenous people in resistance to oil companies in the Amazon, mainly in the region of Archidona in the province of Napo. He is currently involved in Casita del Arbol, a radical community centre in Quito.

7. **Christian Guerrero** is originally from Ecuador, works with Rising Tide Mexico, a chapter of Rising Tide North America. They take a grassroots approach to climate justice by making it applicable on a local level. They are trying to give alternative responses to climate change, opposing the many false solutions that are currently unchallenged. He is also working to make sure that reactionary responses to various policies/projects are articulated within a climate justice mindset. We met him at a meeting of the Rising Tide Network during the conference.

8. **Leonardo Cerdo** is a young indigenous Ecuadorian working with the Federation of Indigenous Association of the Amazon to educate about the evils of the oil companies as well as sustainable alternatives. Both student and activist, he is also involved in other groups including Marea Creciente (Rising Tide) Ecuador. We met him in Quito, Ecuador in 2009, and again at the conference during a meeting of the Rising Tide Network.

9. **Jack Herranen** is from eastern Tennessee, US, a region with many coal mining and mountain top removal. He moved to Bolivia in 1999. Jack and his wife participate in the network RED Aputinari, which is the name of the highest local peak, made up of activists, artists and students. They formed in response to a violent clash in Cochabamba, on 11 January, 2005 where young, right wing, proto-fascist groups openly attacked campesinos and indigenous folk that were marching through the city. They reflect among others on the dynamics of development, the confused notions of poverty and progress, and on the land based values of this region, what people refer to as the 'Andean cosmo-vision.'

10. **Sabu Kohso** is from Japan but lives in New York, US. He was involved in the No G8 Action/Anti-capitalist Forum. We met him at the workshop at the CMPCC on migration and climate change.

11. **Laura Lopez**, works with the Committee for Human Rights in Latin America (Comité para Derechos Humanos en América Latina) in Montreal, Canada. This organisation is involved in denouncing the impacts of mega-projects in Latin America like hydroelectric power plants, mining and oil projects in indigenous territories which have negative impacts on their communities. They are striving to defend the environmental, social and cultural rights of peoples. She is working with a community that has been criminalised and displaced to make place for a uranium mine and is researching the impacts of mining in Canada. We met her at Mesa 18.

12. **Marcela Olivera** is coordinator for the 'Water for All' campaign. After graduating from the university in Cochabamba, Marcela worked for four years as the key international liaison for the 'Coalition for the Defense of Water and Life'. In 2004, she moved to Washington, DC for one year to work for the Water for All campaign, developing the network Red Vida, an inter-American citizens' network on water rights, which she continues to coordinate from Cochabamba. Red Viva assists water rights groups throughout the region to coordinate efforts to preserve or establish the water as a pubic good and human right. Marcela has also worked as a lead researcher at the Democracy Center, a San Francisco and Cochabamba-based NGO. We met Marcela through a contact who had previously spent time in Cochabamba.

13. **Colin Rajah** is the coordinator of the International Migrant Rights Program at the National Network for Immigrant and Refugee Rights (NNIRR). A native of, and political refugee from Malaysia, Rajah has been a community organiser and educator for 2 decades. Colin is part of the Coordinating Committee for the upcoming U.S. Social Forum. He also coordinates the relationships with international migrant organizations especially with Geneva-based Migrants Rights International (MRI), a global network of migrant rights organizations. Colin is author of Malaysia's New Economic Policy: A Case-Study of Elite Economics and has published dozens of articles on working class youth of color, global solidarity education, community development, trade and globalization, as well as on Asia, Southeast Asia and Malaysia specifically. We met Colin when he was talking on the same panel as one of us on Climate Migrants at the CMPCC.

14. **Mayeli Sánchez** is part of the collective 'Acción Directa Autogestiva' (Self-organised direct action) in Puebla, Mexico. Her collective works at the local level on environmental issues. They fight against the repressive government of Puebla. She is also part of the network 'Diálogo y Convención Climática de los Pueblos', which is a grassroots network discussing and organizing towards Cancún (cop-16.org.mx/). We met Mayeli through another Rising Tide contact from Ecuador.

15. **Sankofahamu Sankofa** from Ghana are part of the SANKOFAHAMU Climate Camp planning group (the camp will be held in the third quarter of 2010 in the village of Atidze, in the Volta Region of Ghana). Unfortunately they were financially unable to attend the conference, despite funding from the UK Camp for Climate Action. They asked to spend the money on local activities, but were very keen to still be connected and in touch with the international climate justice movement. We were put in touch with this group through a Ghanaian friend and colleague.

16. **Togbe Kosi Akposoe** is officially the Chair of the group organising the SANKOFAHAMU Climate Camp. Togbe Akposoe is the "Sohefia", that is, the Community Advocate-in-Chief of the Atidze village of the township of Tanyigbe, in the Volta Region of Ghana. Togbe Akposoe himself is mainly a family peasant-farmer who shares with the renowned Asafobaatan Komla Dwamena leadership of the ADIEYIEKUAFO Network of Positive Action Farmers in Ghana. While representing TANUSROHA in the leadership of the GHANADIKAN Cooperative Network of Social Enterprise Action Learning, Togbe Kosi Akposoe also represents ADIEYIEKUAFO in the leadership of the broader West-Afrika-wide umbrella alliance of the ADIEYIEMANFO Movement of Positive Action Networks.

17. **Kojo Prah Annan** is officially the General Secretary of the group organising the SANKOFAHAMU Climate Camp. Kojo progressed in grassroots youth activism within the ranks of the Ghana Chapter of the Youth Concern Global Network (YCGN) and the Planet Repairs Youth Positive Action Campaign (PRYPAC) into broader Community Activism, becoming the current President of the PANAFRIKANYEMEI Cooperative Society for Community Regeneration. He is involved in the Kpong Ressettlement Action Group for Community Regeneration (KRAGCOR) and the GHANADIKAN Network and represents PANAFRIKANYEMEI in the leadership of the ADIEYIEMANFO Movement of Positive Action Networks, which is regarded as the main organisational and mass mobilization backbone of the SANKOFAHAMU Climate Camp.

18. **Awurabaasima Afitsufe Ampofo**, popularly titled "Awura" in short, is officially the Treasurer of the group organising the SANKOFAHAMU Climate Camp. Awura Afitsufe works mainly as a Teacher in the GYE NYAME Ecology Educational Complex (GYE NYAME Ecoducomplex – GNE), in Pokuase, Accra; and also serves as a Joint Coordinating Registrar of the OKRAKE SoulRoots Educational Complex of Lifelong Learning (OKRAKE-SRECOLL). She is also active within the GHANADIKAN Network.

19. **Awura Afitsufe** is a founding member and Principal Organising Secretary of the ADZEWAGBETO Pan-Afrikan Women's Liberation Union. She represents ADZEWAGBETO in the leadership organs of both the ADIEYIEMANFO Movement of Positive Action Networks and the ASASEYAAMMA Pan-Afrikan Green Campaign for Global Justice, among numerous other networks and campaigns operating locally, nationally and internationally.

20. **Severino Sharupe** is from the Achuar nationality, an indigenous people from the Ecuadorian Amazon. He considers himself part of the indigenous movements and, as being part of a community in the Amazon he places himself as the grassroots base of CONAIE (strong indigenous network in Ecuador). We met him at the forests working group and engaged with him in several debates during the two-days discussions.

21. **Soumitra Ghosh** is a researcher and an activist within the National Forum of Forest Peoples and Forest Workers – NFFPFW, India.

BUILDING BRIDGES COLLECTIVE.

We are an ad-hoc group made up of eight people that came together through our shared interest in the CMPCC, put in touch with each other through friends and contacts. We are: Yamine Brien, Jeremy Crowle-Smith, Joanna Cabello, Alice Cutler, Mooness Davarian, Merel de Buck, Chris Kitchen and Bertie Russell. As individuals we are involved with various groups and networks including Rising Tide, No Borders, Climate Justice Action, Camp for Climate Action, Carbon Trade Watch, Somos Sur and Trapese Popular Education Collective. However, the thoughts, analyses and perspectives in this booklet are ours and do not, of course, represent the views of these groups or networks.